Your New Lenses are Ready for Pick Up

A Guide to Seeing the Lighter Side of Life

SUSAN STEWART

YOUR NEW LENSES
ARE READY FOR PICK UP
A Guide to Seeing the Lighter Side of Life

Printed in Canada 2014

ISBN 978-0-9920683-1-8

Publisher: Live Well, Laugh Lots
Toronto, Ontario, Canada

Printer: Ball Media Book Factory
Brantford, Ontario, Canada

Photos: Embrace Photography

Cover Design: Heather Manning

For Shana.

The light of my life.

"When you change the way you look at things, the things you look at change."

- Dr. Wayne Dyer

Contents

Introduction 1

one
Why Seeing The Lighter Side Of Life Is Worth The Bother 11

two
A Caution About The Self-Improvement Movement 39

three
When It Comes To Seeing The Lighter Side Of Life, There Is Nothing To Learn (Recognizing The "Zen Master" You Truly Are) 49

four
Seeing Nothing As Stress 57

five
Seeing Nothing As Stressful 65

six
The Female Brain Versus The Male Brain (Why We Stress About The Stuff That We Do And Why The Reasons Are Different) 75

seven
Noticing How Good You've Got It 87

eight
Put Down Your Crystal Ball 99

nine
How To Cure A Case Of The "Shoulds" 107

ten
Accepting The "Flux Of Life": Seeing The Lighter Side Of Change 119

eleven
Exercise (bear with me…this will be quick and relatively pain-free, I promise) 129

twelve
Be Here Now 137

thirteen
Why It Is Best To Always Be The Hero (The Fine Art Of Re-Framing Your Struggles) 145

fourteen
Keep Your Eyes Off The Prize: Positive Psychology 101 151

fifteen
Crisis or Opportunity? It Depends On How You Look At It… 161

sixteen
Seeing The "Good" In Everyone 167

seventeen
Do You See The Magic Even When Things Don't Seem So Magical? 177

eighteen
Leave The Rescuing To The Cops, Firefighters, And Lifeguards 187

nineteen
Seeing Struggle As The Required Tension In Your Life 193

twenty
Try Giving Up All Hope 201

twenty-one
What If Life Was A Game? (Life Viewed Through The Lens Of A Spiritual Warrior) 207

Introduction

I want to start off with a disclaimer. The purchase of this book does not include an actual set of new eyeglasses. I'm pretty sure you interpreted the title of this book to be a cute metaphor, but I don't want you to feel sad when you reach the end of the book and realize it didn't come with a redeemable coupon for a set of designer specs. You experiencing a major letdown (and potential downward spiral into an emotional rabbit hole) due to a simple misunderstanding like that is something I definitely want to avoid given that this book is aimed at helping you lighten up.

In lieu of actual new lenses, you will be offered all kinds of ways to see the lighter side of the changes and challenges that unfold in life. The various perspectives contained in this book (the "lenses that are ready for pick up") are a reminder of the freedom you were born with – the freedom of choice. You always have a choice about how you view things and that choice influences how you think about and respond to things.

This book explores how to exercise your freedom of choice through the practice of being deliberate with your perceptions and thoughts. In other words, selecting your lenses involves consciously choosing how you view and think about everything and everyone around you. The practice of being deliberate with your perceptions and thoughts can be quite powerful as the lenses through which you view things almost entirely determines your experience.

This book was inspired by a profound life lesson I learned the hard way. About ten years ago, I quit stand-up comedy because I was miserable in the business. I loved performing comedy, however, I was no fan of the business of comedy and the comedy club culture. As I began pursuing the dream of "making it big", my head began to fill with self-doubt, fear, and a longing for something better. A few years into my comedy career, my unease developed into anxiety and depression that made getting on stage and being funny pretty much impossible. I took a six month break from performing that seemed to revive my self-belief and resiliency, but about year after that, the demons were back in full force and I made the decision to quit comedy for good.

I quit stand-up thinking that leaving comedy would solve everything. I thought that if I went somewhere else and did something else, the unease in my life would just magically disappear. I thought that if I left and got a "real job" I would be happier. I was convinced that by changing my external circumstances, my daily experience would improve.

Have you ever done that? Have you ever realized that you're miserable and decided to change your external circumstances thinking that would improve your daily experience? Maybe one day you woke up and said, "*Screw it. I'm out of here.*" Maybe you said that to your first husband or wife, but that is none of my business so I'll move on to the next part of my story.

Where was I? Oh yes, I quit comedy for good. But the thing was, I had no back-up plan. After I left comedy, I had no new job to go to. The fact that I quit something that I loved and thought I would do for the rest of life without any idea of what I was going to do next clearly indicates just how miserable I was. Thankfully, when one door shuts another door opens. Thankfully, endings are also beginnings. Thankfully, I wasn't playing in the traffic for very long.

Shortly after quitting stand-up comedy, I landed a job working in a Human Resources department in the Ontario Government. Now, I know what you are thinking. I went from stand-up comedy to *sit-down* comedy. You may not have been thinking that, but chances are good that you are thinking that I couldn't have changed up my external circumstances anymore if I tried. Yes, everything around me was different. My workplace culture was very different. My job responsibilities were very different. The *lighting* was very different. However, even though everything around me was different, I was still in the same miserable place because the lenses through which I was viewing things had not changed. The experience created out of my negative perceptions and thoughts was all very familiar.

The profound life lesson I learned as I sat there in my "real job" no happier than when I did stand-up comedy is perfectly captured in the title of a book by Jon Kabat-Zinn, *Where Ever You Go, There You Are.*

Where ever I went, there I was. Where ever I went, there I was wearing a certain set of lenses and those lenses delivered a certain experience whether I was performing stand-up comedy or working in a Human Resources department in the Ontario Government.

Since realizing the significant role I play in my experience, I have become a passionate seeker of ways to lighten up. Being mindful of how I see and think about things has become a powerful practice in my life because, as my story rather clearly illustrates, seeing the lighter side of life does not come easy for me.

Yes, that's right. Even though I used to be a stand-up comic, seeing the lighter side of life does not come easy for me. I'm not like *those* people. You know *those* people. *Those* people who are always calm, always in a good mood, always have their sense of humour on hand, and always have something positive say when everyone else is freaking right out. You know *those* people. All hell could be breaking loose and there they go floating by on a white, fluffy cloud of optimism smiling away. I call those happy, optimists of the world, the “floaters”. When “floaters” take a step backward in life, right after taking a step forward, they don’t see it as a disaster. Nah, they see it more like the cha-cha.

I am not a floater. I’ve never been a floater and I will probably never be a floater. I’m in the other category. I am what I call a “worker”. I have to work at this happiness thing. In light of the fact that you are reading this book, I suspect that you are a fellow “worker”. I suppose you could be a “floater” interested in a bunch of affirmations that confirm that you are indeed just that good at being happy, but I’m putting my money on you being a “worker”.

Being a “worker” just means that you have to dig much deeper to appear, look, sound, or feel like a “floater.” In case you are not sure whether or not you are a “worker”, I have listed below some classic signs to help you determine your disposition.

You know you're a "worker" when…

- You see someone at work laughing, smiling, and really enjoying themselves and you assume they must be on some good drugs you don't know about or they are having an affair.

- Some days the person you're the most tired of being around is you.

- You post cryptic negative status updates (such as "WTF?!?!") on Facebook alluding to your angst, but not feeling comfortable enough to reveal the details about why you are once again sweating the small stuff.

- You dance like everyone is watching…and judging you harshly.

- You tell someone that you are happy for them, but you don't really mean it because you're having a hard enough time being happy about the good things in your own life.

- The last time you tried to meditate, you made your grocery list.

- You believe all the things you tell yourself late at night.

- You have read or watched *Eat, Pray, Love* more than once.

- You stand in front of your bathroom mirror in the morning and give yourself a motivational pep talk. "Today I am going to keep it together. I'm not going to lose it. No matter what anyone says to me!"

- You have been known to demonstrate road rage while driving home from yoga class.

- You recited the Serenity Prayer the last time you were asked to say grace before a meal.

If you are indeed a fellow "worker", then welcome to my world and welcome to what will be an exploration of why and how to do the "work". The "work" of exercising your freedom of choice and choosing to see challenges in ways that lift you up rather than bring you down. I liken the effort of being deliberate with your perceptions and thoughts to the effort you make to "be on your game" during a job interview or a hot date. As you sit there with the hope of employment or love, you are completely self-aware and insistent on shining as brightly as you can – every perception and thought you create is based on that strong intention. Being "on my game" and carefully choosing how I look at things has become a powerful practice in my life and one that I pursue each and every day. To be quite honest, if I let my thoughts run wild, I would quickly become a depressed and anxious inspirational author and speaker.

The "work" involved in seeing the lighter side of life is also known as the practice of self-awareness, mindfulness, and consciousness. Call it what you want – it doesn't matter which one you choose because they all involve the same practice of paying attention and noticing how you're responding at any given moment. This practice places you in a kind of "awakened" state that has most likely saved you from flatulating in the middle of a yoga class. If you have ever done yoga, then you know you have to work at that – you have to be on your game.

One of the main reasons we struggle to see the lighter side of life is because we're so busy. Isn't it ironic that we seem to be busier now than when we had to churn our own butter? I mean, come on, those were some really busy days. Back in the pioneer times, if you wanted anything, you first had to make it. They had to grow their own food, make their own clothes, and build their own homes. They even had to make their own candles and not for the sexy reasons, but rather, to avoid walking into things at night. Without candles, the poor things couldn't even find their way to their bedroom. That is when we were busy. Nowadays, if we have to take the car in for an oil change, drop off the dry cleaning, pick up stuff at Costco, and exchange something at The Gap, all while trying to keep the kids from killing each other over who's turn it is to play on the iPad, we have reached our limit. We simply can't take on one more thing.

Maybe we're taking things too seriously because we've gone a bit soft – especially those precious people who always seem to have a full plate. Do you know someone precious like that? Someone who, no matter what's going on in their life, seems to always have a full plate. Every time you see them they go on and on about having a full plate. Here's a question – how big is their plate? I think there might be some people walking around with teeny, tiny plates. Of course their plate is full – it came with an Easy Bake Oven.

For whatever reason you might find yourself taking life too seriously, I am excited to offer you this collection of ideas. These different ways of seeing the lighter side of changes and challenges can help you live with more ease and reap the rewards of a positive outlook.

Before I conclude this introduction, I would like to point out that I did not write this book with the expectation that reading this book would convert you from a "worker" (assuming you are one) into a "floater". This book does not have mastery in mind. Mindfulness is a practice and you will most likely have to "work" at seeing the lighter side of life for the rest of your life. The ideas presented in this book are here to help you catch yourself in the act of taking things too seriously so you can make the choice to view things in a way that will change your experience because…. “where ever you go, there you are”.

One

Why Seeing The Lighter Side Of Life Is Worth The Bother

Because seeing the lighter side of life often requires a bit of effort, here are some reasons why carefully selecting your lenses is worth the "work".

Reason #1: The Mind-Body Connection

In a nutshell, how you see things creates your mindset and your mindset directly impacts your health.

Every feeling produces a thought and every thought has a chemical equivalent. The relationship between how we respond to something and our hormone levels is often called, the mind-body connection. When your outlook is positive and you are feeling good, your body produces re-energizing, relaxing, and immune-system-boosting hormones (commonly known as endorphins), such as dopamine and serotonin. When your outlook is negative and you are feeling stressed, your body produces stress hormones such as norepinephrine and cortisol. When stress hormone levels are high (and endorphin levels are low) for an extended period of time, there are harmful effects on your body including a weakened immune system, inflammation, and hypertension.

Now let's take a look at the health benefits of stress...

Yes, those are all the good things that chronic stress does for your body.

Chronic stress is that stress that lingers for days, weeks, months, or (if you are the leader of the free world or married to the wrong person) years.

This may seem controversial or just plain confusing because you may have heard that there are some benefits to stress.

There is a form of stress that serves a purpose in your life, but it's the short-lived stress that you only experience for a few seconds, minutes, or hours. This short burst of stress (the fight-or-flight response) is the instinct we have from the beginning of human civilization when the only cause to be frazzled was because of real danger. The release of adrenaline came with a decision to literally put up your dukes or run screaming.

This instinct (and the release of adrenaline) is what now helps us rise to the occasion when we face a real or perceived threat. Whether or not the danger is real, we still experience a rapid increase in our levels of concentration, strength, and energy. If making your bed typically leaves you feeling winded, this short-lived stress would give you the adrenaline rush you'd need to stand a chance in a UFC match. I guess in a way, this short-lived stress can lengthen your life because if you ever facing a real danger, then remaining alive is totally good for your health.

And let's be honest, there are many times that short-lived stress helps you rise to the occasion when you are not physically threatened, but you *feel* threatened in some other way. Your concentration level is sky-high when you give a speech at a wedding or a presentation at work. That ability to "perform" when it is "show time" is the survival instinct that makes short-lived stress useful in our lives. It's precisely why you were able to come up with a valid reason for missing your curfew when your parents caught you sneaking in late at night.

So, okay, there are some good things about short-lived stress, but in these modern times when we are often facing perceived threats (rather than physical threats), the fight-or-flight response is more likely helping you to save face rather than save your life.

But unless you find yourself facing real danger on a regular basis, there are no health benefits associated with chronic stress.

Back in my stand-up comedy career, my prolonged periods of despair altered my chemical levels for so long that it caused me to experience anxiety and depression. Mental illness is a symptom of chronic stress. While it can come with physical effects, it has its own unique set of cognitive challenges such as loss of memory, lack of concentration, and paranoia. The changes in behaviour that are experienced with depression and anxiety are just another indication that the body is being affected by stressful thinking.

When I was dealing with my third depression in three years, my mom said to me, "*You know, Sue. I get so worried when you get like this because as you spend so much time in the darkness, it's going to end up shortening your life.*" I looked at her, smiled, and thanked her for the pick-me-up.

In her subtle and gentlest of ways, what my mom said to me that day was true. Those nasty stress hormones at a high level in my body for so long were not only causing me mental distress, but would eventually weaken me physically. Interesting how that word, "dis-ease", accurately reflects that the body is responding to a lack of ease.

Because the mind-body connection can also work in our favour, when we live with ease, there is ease in the body which promotes strong health and longevity. In his book, *You! The Owner's Manual*, Dr. Oz states that people who maintain a positive mindset live 1.7 to 8 years longer than their stressed-out counterparts. Now, I know what you are thinking, but don't go telling those certain people that you know that they are going to die an untimely death. That won't help lighten things up for them one bit.

Managing The Mind-Body Connection

Whether it is short-lived or chronic stress, the release of stress hormones happens whenever your body senses danger based on how you are feeling in response to your environment. The tricky part is that you end up indicating to your body that you are in danger when there is both *real* danger and *perceived* danger. Real danger is running out of a burning building while perceived danger is running around worried about moving out of your building next month. When you feel stressed, no matter what the cause, your body interprets that feeling as danger and stress hormones are released whether or not you are actually in danger.

When I used to work in an office building, the fire alarm system would sometimes go off without any mention of a scheduled drill. My colleagues and I would immediately become worried and start scrambling around to collect our valuables. A few minutes later we'd all be ushered down the stairwell and outside. After about twenty minutes of standing outside anxiously staring at the sky looking for signs of smoke, we would be told that it was a false alarm. Our response to the false alarm was much like how it would have been if it was a real emergency.

When we launch our bodies into the stress response without any real danger at hand, that is like being in a state of "false alarm". A situation may not warrant the stress response (as our lives are not really being threatened) and yet what we put ourselves through physically, mentally, and emotionally has the same level of intensity.

Our body's inability to decipher between real danger and perceived danger (a "false alarm") is what I call the mind-body connection's "flaw in the system". Your body is not smart enough to filter your feelings and the sense of danger it receives. Your body can't be selective and hold off the release of stress hormones when you're viewing and thinking about something in a way that is placing yourself in a state of "false alarm". To your body, all danger is created equal and all danger is real. Considering how often we feel stressed, our bodies must think we're quite brave to leave our homes each day.

When you are deliberate about how you view and think about challenging circumstances, you are able to manage the mind-body connection's "flaw in the system". By seeing the lighter side of life, you are also telling your body that you are not in danger.

The chain reaction of feeling-thought-chemical release is explored in a revolutionary TED talk, by psychologist Kelly McGonigal. Dr. McGonigal shares new research that suggests that stress may only be bad for you if you believe that to be the case. If you interpret the symptoms of stress (heart pounding, rapid and shallow breathing, sweating, etc.) as positive, you can avoid experiencing the harmful effects of stress that weaken your health. If you ever start displaying symptoms of being stressed about something, try feeling excited about it and thinking it's a good thing. As it turns out, along with your body's inability to detect when danger is real or not, it also doesn't know when you're faking it.

Reason #2: "Waist Management"

A common effect of chronic stress is an increase in appetite. As you struggle along with your head spinning in all kinds of directions, the urge to eat everything in sight is typically high and your willpower to resist that urge is low which often results in you consuming more food. On the other hand, the fight-or-flight response causes the opposite reaction. As you suddenly swerve your car to avoid a collision, your first instinct is probably not to head to a drive-thru.

If you consume more food when you are stressed, it's probably safe to assume that you aren't gobbling down tons of big ol' salads. No, chances are you're making a date with a bag of cookies, a tub of ice cream, or a chocolate bar. Yes, you are most likely craving carbohydrates which is just a fancy, scientific name for sugar.

This craving for sugar is caused by cortisol rising in response to stress. Cortisol basically takes us by the hand and walks us straight to the comfort food. As it turns out, cortisol, is the most potent appetite signal your body produces – its main function is to make you ravenous. At the beginning of human civilization, stress was connected to circumstances that were truly life-threatening (real danger) like being chased by some cranky (and hungry) sabre-tooth tiger. In response to the physical threat, cortisol was produced, which in turn, released sugar in the bloodstream. When you're being chased by a wild animal, a shot of glucose is very useful as you can expend a great deal of energy running for your life. The hunger felt later (from all the insulin in the body causing a low amount of blood sugar) was a natural reaction to the physical feat and a necessary reminder to refuel for the next chase.

Fast forward to the 21st century when most people's stress is related to modern pressures such as work deadlines and traffic jams. We have the same amount of cortisol coursing through our bloodstreams without the part where we run for our lives. The release of cortisol yanks down our blood sugar which triggers a craving for food. However, since there is no reason to expend any physical energy for survival, those extra calories don't get used. In the rat race, rather than our lives being threatened, it's our waist lines.

Undeniably, there is a real connection between chronically being stressed and chronically consuming lots of sugar. If you ask me, it's rather appropriate that the word, “STRESSED” spelled backwards is, “DESSERTS”.

If you ever want to gauge your stress level quickly, simply reach down and feel your thighs.

Now, that was mostly a joke because what typically happens is that we don’t tend to store much fat from sugar in our thighs. Once our bloodstream reaches the maximum amount of sugar it can contain, the sugar starts getting stored as fat in various part of the body, mainly the abdominal region. With excessive belly fat, you may find yourself sporting a “sugar tire” or “muffin top”. It was once referred to me as a “bird bath” which sounded very odd at the time, but after some visualization, I got it. Feel free to take a moment to do your own visualization if you need to.

Call it what you want, but the fact is belly fat is really the only fat on the body that is a direct threat to your health as it can raise your blood pressure and your cholesterol levels. If you have a little “junk in the trunk” or a pair of “BINGO arms” (that may require some visualization as well, but probably not as much), those soft spots are not as big of a concern as they don’t negatively affect your well-being. They may affect your chances of getting a hot date or feeling groovy on a nude beach, but they won't hinder your health like belly fat. The best way to keep a healthy heart is to have a healthy waist size. For women, 35 inches or less is a healthy waist size. As for men, they get a few more inches. Just one more thing, hey? Yes, for men, a waist size of up to 40 inches is considered healthy.

Not everyone consumes more food when they are stressed, though. You know some of those people, don't you? That's right, they're the drinkers. Or they are the non-eaters. When they get stressed, their appetite goes right out the window and they hardly eat a thing for days or weeks. That's what I like to call a "crisis diet". You're an emotional wreck, but damn you look good.

Reason #3: The *Other* Energy Crisis

You mostly likely have heard of the global energy crisis which pertains to the planet's depletion of natural energy sources due to industrial development and population growth. Basically, the world's energy supply is far less than the demand. Well, move over David Suzuki, because there is more than one energy crisis going on. The energy supply of humans is being drained by our incessant "mind-chatter". Our negative and stressful thoughts can demand more of our energy than we can produce. The bottom line is that it takes a great deal of effort to be stressed.

You know stress is slowing you down when you finally make it to the end of the week and there you are on Friday night at home fast asleep on the couch by nine o'clock. That's sexy.

We tend to think that our energy levels are determined by our age. I often hear adults say, "*I just don't have the energy I used to.*" While I don't think it's reasonable to expect a geriatric to keep up the pace of a teenager, I do think there is a lot of fatigue getting unfairly blamed on a number. This *other* energy crisis that many of us face is really just an accessibility issue. When you are older, you still have energy, but sometimes you just can't get to it because your energy is being used to fuel all the fretting. While your energy could be flowing freely and dispersed in many directions, all routes head north to sustain all the chatter going on in your head. For the most part, many of us still have the energy we used to, it's just a matter of whether or not we can lighten up and free up that energy for good use.

Unless you are over 80 years old, you do have a significant amount of energy. I want you to reflect on how you feel and behave when you take a vacation. Look at you and all of your energy. Look at you able to access all of your energy because you have a quiet mind. Look at you having a quiet mind because your attention is fully placed on the present moment. There you are on that tropical holiday walking miles and miles of a beach every morning to start your day. There you are in that big, cosmopolitan city marching up and down the streets as you shop for 8 to 10 hours while holding approximately 12 to 14 shopping bags! "*No! We can't stop for lunch! We have to keep going!*" There you are exploring little European towns trudging up and down the cobblestone hills like a champion! Look at you accessing all of your energy!

Then you get back to work. Your mind starts chattering away again. And you are so tired. You can hardly muster up the chutzpah to go to the bathroom. After a brief deliberation, you think to yourself, "*Screw it, I'll go at lunch. I have to go in that direction anyway.*"

Sometimes this *other* energy crisis is linked to insomnia. We're tired because our "mind-chatter" has kept us up all night. We lay there in bed wide awake until the wee hours of the morning thinking about every challenging thing going on in our lives right now. We wonder what she meant when she said that. We decide that we're failing as a parent. We are certain that we won't get that new job we want.

Back in my Human Resources career, I would lay awake in bed obsessing about all the things I had to do the next day. It was hard not to be tired the next day after being up until four o'clock in the morning running through the to-do list that was sitting on my desk at work. And God forbid I suddenly remembered something I had to do the next day that wasn't on my to-do list. Upon that stunning realization, I would lie awake thinking incessantly about that one task to implant it into my subconscious so it would be the first thing on my mind in the morning. Some nights I would be so desperate to get some sleep that I would call myself at work and leave a reminder message. Without fail, I started the message (that I leaving for myself) with a greeting. After the tone, I would say, "*Hi, it's me.*" Well, I didn't want to just start barking orders at myself – I got that from enough people during the day. And then, without fail, I would end off by saying, "*Ok. Have a nice day!*" I figured it would probably be the only time I would hear it all day. I left the corporate world in 2008 so I realize the technology has evolved since then. You may not be calling yourself at all, but that's because you're emailing yourself – which is fine until you start replying.

Whether it is the "daytime drain" or insomnia (or both), the key to solving the *other* energy crisis is seeing things in your life in ways that allows you to be present. When you are present, your mind is quiet and when your mind is quiet, look at you and all of your energy!

Reason #4: The "Human Energy Hoover"

Speaking of energy, everything on the planet is energy and every person on this planet is energy. Some are denser than others, but hey, you can't pick your family. Whether it's living or not, every form of energy (at a molecular level) is constantly moving or more specifically, vibrating. Everything and everyone is producing vibrations which are commonly referred to as "vibes". The quality of a human's energy (the level of our "vibes") is influenced by our thoughts.

Positive thoughts produce positive (or high) vibrations and negative thoughts produce negative (or low) vibrations.

Seeing the lighter side of life is worth the effort because the "vibes" you produce are contagious. What you think and say can influence other people's energy.

It may not actually be energy that is contagious. It may be the mood that produces the energy that is contagious. In his book, The Happiness Advantage, positive psychology expert, Shawn Achor, explains that studies have shown that when three strangers meet in a room, the most emotionally expressive person transmits his or her mood on to the others within just two minutes. This phenomenon is explained by neuroscience. In our brains we have these things called "mirror neurons" that are located next to "motor neurons". The close proximity between these neurons lead us to copy people's feelings and actions. As we observe someone's mood, a mirror neuron fires and then a motor neuron "mirrors" the behaviour being observed. Finally, an explanation for why some couples wear matching windbreakers.

Whether your neurons are playing tricks on you or someone is messing with your "vibes", it's tough to dispute that another person's negative mindset can bring you down.

Have you ever worked with somebody who was not having a very good day? That was a long day, wasn't it? They walked around all day wearing the "face". You know the "face". The "face" is a unique combination of looking angry and looking like you are working through a severe gas pain. And they didn't say a single word all day, did they? They didn't have to! It was pure and totally uncomfortable silence except for when they would emit a large sigh every time they walked by you. The "face", working in conjunction with the deadly silence (intermittently broken by inaudible moans and groans), can generate negative energy that has the ability to tear through a place like wildfire. And that negative energy is not only fast and powerful, but it can also remove all the positive energy within a 250 meter radius. Beware of the "Human Energy Hoover" because it is no fun working with someone who sucks.

It is important to keep in mind that no one is a "Hoover" on purpose. I really don't think anyone ever actually intends to put out negative energy and transmit their mood on to others. Okay, right now you might be coming up with a short list of names, but stay with me here. I really don't think there is anyone who ever wakes up in the morning and, as they get ready for work, devises a mastermind plan precisely calculating how they will successfully drag down every single person who crosses their path throughout their day. I really don't think anyone brushes their teeth thinking, "*Sharing my misery is going to be so much fun! They have no idea what's coming today! I'm gonna make that one lady cry!"* While I don't think any act of a "Hoover" is premeditated, I do think taking life too seriously, and dispensing negative "vibes" every which way, can happen to anybody.

By carefully selecting your lenses, not only are you allowing yourself to live with more ease, but you are also being responsible for the energy you bring to every space.

Never underestimate the impact your energy has on other people because let's be honest, everybody brings joy to a room...either by entering or exiting.

Reason #5: You Are Basically A Magnet With Shoes On

While energy's contagious quality may be debatable, the magnetism of energy starts and ends with our "vibes". I am referring to something called "The Law of Attraction" which is the belief that energy attracts "like" energy. Again, thoughts are energy and depending on the quality of your thoughts, you are sending out positive or negative "vibes". Those "vibes" go out and attract people, events, and circumstances with similar "vibes". Whether or not you are aware of this particular "law", you have most likely experienced the magnetism of energy.

You know those days when things are easy, you are on top of your game, and you have lots of fun? Those days when your outlook is bright and you think all kinds of positive things and say all kinds of positive things. As you are thinking and saying all those positive things, more positive things happen. Things are getting done! People are agreeable, attentive, and punctual! Success is a constant outcome! At any point during days like that, do you ever turn to someone and say, "*I'm on a roll!*"? Or perhaps you have said those very words during a game when you could do no wrong, or in the midst of a great week at work, or when another one of your selfies brings down Twitter. You have probably said, "*I'm on a roll!*" at one time or another. Whether or not your positive mindset was first influenced by positive circumstances, it was your positive energy that resulted in more positive things.

Let's now flip it around and reflect on the days when you thought maybe you were on some kind of morbid candid camera reality show being set up for a bunch of tragedies so other people could feel better about their lives. The "Law of Attraction" is constantly at work and it doesn't pick and choose what thoughts we pay attention to. As my favourite "Law of Attraction" author/guru, Michael Losier, says, "*You get what you focus on whether you like it or not.*"

Have you ever had a day when you were pissed off and you hadn't even gotten to work yet? When you did arrive, you walked around all day thinking negative things and saying negative things. That day everything was difficult. Nothing got done. People were disagreeable, disengaged, and no one was on time for anything. The technology broke down, the network was on the fritz, and the photocopier was jammed again. On a day like that, did you ever turn to someone and say, "*I'm on a roll!*"? You probably didn't, but what you were witnessing was the magnetism of your energy just like on those other great days.

I experienced the not-so-good kind of roll when I visited a public washroom at a mall. I can't stand using public washrooms – especially at malls. I was at the mall with a friend, but lucky her, she didn't have to go, so I headed to the washroom alone and I wasn't happy about it. As I made my way to the washroom, I was muttering all kinds of negative things to myself. I walked into the washroom and yes, you guessed it, there was a line-up for the stalls. The day a women's public washroom has the supply that meets the demand will be a great day. After what felt like an eternity, my turn finally came and I ran toward the free stall. I swung the door shut only to find that the lock was broken. I wasn't about to get back into line so I placed my right hand on the door to keep it closed. So there I am trying to take off my pants with one hand. Always a treat. I then proceeded to hang my purse on the back of the door on the hook…that was missing. So there I was squatting over the toilet with one hand pressed on the door and my purse hanging around my neck. If you have ever assumed this position, or something like it, you know that it is quite a workout – not all that different from an advanced version of a yoga pose. Naturally, the burning in my quadriceps made me grumble some more.

A few moments later, I reached for some toilet paper and wouldn't you know it, there was none left. I had to ask the lady in the stall beside me to kindly pass me some, which is about as much fun as buying feminine hygiene products when there's a dude working the cash.

Once I was done in the stall, I walked out and headed to the sink to wash my hands. The sinks were the kind with those motion sensors that turn on the water, but no matter how hard I tried, the sensor somehow didn't sense that I was waving my hands and flailing my arms all around. I tried the one on the left. Nothing. I tried the one on the right. Nothing again. I tried everything to get these faucets to work, but quite frankly, it was starting to look and feel more like foreplay than anything else.

I was on a roll.

I finally gave up and decided to go and buy some hand disinfectant instead. Demonstrating a keen sense of irony, as I headed towards the door to leave, water began rushing out of all three faucets. I dove back to one of the sinks and sweet hallelujah, I washed my hands. I then walked over to the paper towel dispenser...which was empty. I stood there with wet hands and then I decided to do what any self-respecting woman would do in that situation. I used my hair.

As I walked toward my friend who was waiting for me, I noticed that she was looking down at my feet and grinning. I gazed down and there was a piece of toilet paper trailing from my left foot. I looked at her and said, "*Now, where the hell was that five minutes ago!*"

This "law" has not been scientifically proven, but odds are you have seen it play out in your life many times. You most likely desire positive things for your future; so your apparent super-power to attract positive things into your life by having a positive mindset is a pretty cool reason that seeing the lighter side of life is with worth the work.

Reason #6: Brain Gain

"75% of job success can be predicted by optimism levels, social support, and the ability to see challenges in a positive light."

- Shawn Achor, *The Happiness Advantage*

This statistic reflects the direct impact our mindset has on the function of our brain. Neuroscience has proven that our brains have the ability to change, otherwise known a neural plasticity. How our brains change is based on how we choose to view and respond to our external circumstances.

With the absence of stressful thoughts and an increase in positive thoughts, we can re-shape and re-wire our brains in ways that improve its function and efficiency. With a positive mindset, new neurons are created, new neural pathways and connections are formed, areas of the brain grow, and communication systems speed up.

The improvement in brain activity that is linked to feeling good has a lot to do with the release of endorphins, which are naturally occurring hormones that re-energize and relax us. That oh-so-beloved calm feeling you get during or after exercise (the relaxation response) is due to your body being flooded by endorphins. Two types of these endorphins (dopamine and serotonin) also turn on the learning centres of our brains. These endorphins help us absorb and organize new information, retain information longer, and retrieve information faster. And because happiness is a choice, the best part is that you can trigger the release of these endorphins any time you want. In fact, neuroscience has proven that when you laugh or smile, your body releases these good feeling chemicals into your bloodstream that are normally very expensive and highly illegal.

Change your lenses. Change your thoughts. Change your brain function. Change your ability to reach your potential.

Somewhat connected to this fancy, scientific brain activity stuff, is another benefit called, "The Ideal Performance State". I bet you have all kinds of memories of performing well at something (sports particularly) and you'll likely recall that you were relaxed and generally feeling good at the time. Sports psychologist, James E. Loehr, coined the term, "The Ideal Performance State". Loehr's book, *The New Toughness Training for Sports,* contains all kinds of evidence from various case studies that prove that a relaxed, positive mindset leads to a higher level of performance in sport. In turn, stress stifles an athlete's ability to reach their potential. The essence of Loehr's theory is that when there is a lack of physical and mental tension, our bodies and minds can do what they know how to do. We essentially "get out of our own way" and our ability shine through.

Being aware of Loehr's research for many years now, I always smile when I hear an athlete being interviewed after winning a game or championship and they tell the reporter how relaxed and at ease they were as they played. I also often hear athletes talk about having fun in the midst of their pursuit of success. After the big win, players regularly reveal that in one way or another, consciously or subconsciously, they had placed themselves in the positive and relaxed mindset that contributes to "The Ideal Performance State".

Perhaps you have seen first-hand the direct relationship between feeling good and performing at a high level in sport. I have definitely seen the connection at work in the sports that I play, but I have also seen the travesty of taking a game way too seriously. And that is precisely why lightening up more on the golf course continues to be a personal goal of mine.

Viewing yourself in a positive light is so important. For example, the other day I was at the dentist and he suggested I get a crown. I said, "*I know. Right?!?*"

Two

A Caution About The Self-Improvement Movement

The conscious decision to see the lighter side of life and generally be a happier, more peaceful, kind, compassionate, loving person is definitely worth the "work", but there is an element of danger as well. That danger is guilt.

As you strive toward being more enlightened, there are times when all spiritual thoughts and Zen behaviours go right out the window. You worry. You feel alone. You judge. You gossip. You interfere. You grasp. You close your heart. You protect your sense of self. You resist what is. You believe your negative thoughts. You lose faith. You take something way too damn seriously. You are anywhere but in the present moment. And then with a heavy sigh, you think to yourself, "*With everything I have read and learned (and all the inspirational quotes I have "liked" and "shared" on Facebook) I should know better by now.*"

And then comes the story in your mind telling you that you're going backwards. "*I'm such a failure. Where did I go wrong*?"

When you slip into self-*un*awareness or abandon your spiritual outlook on life, it can leave you wondering how it could have happened, what you could have missed, or what there is still left to learn. In other words, the desire to be a "better" human being can eclipse self-acceptance.

As you're sitting there in the lotus position trying to focus only on your inhales and exhales, you find yourself making plans for the weekend or replaying a conversation you had with someone earlier that day. As you notice that, yet again, you drifted away from the present moment, you think, "*Damn it. I did it again. I suck at meditating! Bad meditator! Bad meditator!*"

Any book, magazine, audio recording, workshop, and conference to do with self-help, might do well to have a label or a sign warning you about the self-judgement and self-deprecation that may (and probably will) ensue when you face your humanity. *Warning: As you try to improve yourself, you may end up being way more neurotic and critical of yourself than ever before.*

To avoid the "heady-ness" that can arise when wanting to "improve" one's self, I urge you to remember two important things:

1. The goal is not perfection.

Placing an expectation on yourself that you're eventually going to be a non-stop source of love and light and give the Dalai Lama a real run for his money is just plain unrealistic. Even after many years riding the self-improvement train, you are going to go off the tracks once in a while. Inevitably you'll think or do stuff that is far from enlightened, mindful, or spiritual. You'll get jealous. You'll take something personally. As she leaves the room, you'll whisper under your breath, "*What a bitch.*"

You are human and to be human is to be imperfect. To accept and love yourself exactly as you are is the most enlightened thing you can do. However, self-acceptance can be a long and challenging process. Can you accept that at times you'll probably struggle with that too?

In a mediation class I once took, my teacher, Pat, urged us to be extremely gentle on ourselves because focusing on our breath one hundred percent of the time was not actually the goal. The goal of meditation is to notice when thoughts cause you to drift away from the breath because it is that higher level of awareness that meditation helps us to nurture. Pat would remind us that when your mind wanders, don't sit there and beat yourself up, but rather, simply take that as a signal to let go of those thoughts, and begin again.

When you "fall from grace" and slip into old ways of seeing things and thinking about things, don't beat yourself up, just begin again. Change those lenses you are wearing. Your new lenses are always ready for pick up.

2. The goal of being a "better person" is a natural fallout of the self-help movement.

Self-improvement suggests there's something wrong with you, so you're already starting off with a disadvantage. I once spoke at a conference that had the slogan, "A Better Me, A Better You". I was disheartened that the message being conveyed was, "*You aren't good enough just the way you are.*"

The truth is you are enough just the way you are. Anything that suggests that you are sub-standard is just a perception – something completely made-up. You may want to *feel* better, but you don't need to *be* better. You may want to make changes in your life to *feel* better and enjoy your life more, but there is no way you can *be* better.

To add to the irony (and dysfunction) of self-improvement, the best way to feel better, is to realize that you are perfect just the way you are.

Rather than striving toward self-improvement, strive for self-actualization. Self-actualization is about moving away from trying to be your "ideal self" and focusing instead on being your "real self". Research shows that when people live lives that are different from their true nature and capabilities, they are less likely to be happy than those who choose to be authentic.

Screw self-improvement and challenge what you think the world expects of you.

Go back to when you were kid. When you were around seven or eight years old, you declared to the world who you really are. You spoke and lived your truth all day and every day. What excited and bored you back then was a glimpse into what would excite and bore you now. What challenged you then most likely still challenges you (to some degree) now. That playful, loving kid full of wonder and enthusiasm is the real you.

Self-actualization is a process of letting go of the thought patterns and belief systems you have that suggest that you aren't good enough just the way you are. Rather than spending your time being something you are not, because you were fed some story that being someone else was better, spend your time getting rid of whatever has shifted you away from your truth. That person you were when you were a kid didn't have "mind-chatter" that suggested being or doing anything to please other people. With that quiet mind, you not only rocked your truth, but you were free. You were free of any thinking that limited you or limited your joy. When you were a kid, you didn't have any thoughts that suggested you weren't lovely just the way you are. And guess what? You were happier, more peaceful, kind, compassionate, and loving.

You don't need to improve, the only thing you might want to do is be freer by remembering your real self and all your loveliness.

Ditch self-improvement and change your intention to self-actualization. Rather than striving to change who you are, can you uncover the *real* you?

Go on that retreat to remember your loveliness.

Practice yoga to remember your loveliness.

Meditate to remember your loveliness.

Pray, chant, dance, play, breathe, unplug, run, stretch, laugh, get enough sleep to remember that you are lovely just the way you are.

Spending time with children has helped me lighten up in many ways – especially about people. The other day, a guy was being really rude and shouting curse words at me. I just remained centred and peaceful and said to him, *"May you step on a piece of Lego."*

Haven't you always found your way? Haven't you always figured it out? Haven't you always gotten back up after a fall? Haven't you always received some kind of gift no matter what the challenge? Haven't you always been guided to what truly is best for you? Why, oh why, would that end now?

Three

When It Comes To Seeing The Lighter Side Of Life, There Is Nothing To Learn (Recognizing The "Zen Master" You Truly Are)

As I mentioned in the introduction, I did stand-up comedy for about five years and then one day I literally woke up in the morning and decided to quit. The reason I quit comedy was because it became increasingly more difficult to be funny when I would spend most of my day listening to, and believing, the negative and fearful thoughts that would play over and over in my head. "*When am I ever going to get it together?!*" "*Nothing ever turns out the way I want it to!*" "*I have absolutely no idea what I'm doing and people are soon going to figure that out!*"

The negative thoughts in my head were like living with an abusive roommate who would tell me lies all day long. Can you imagine living with someone who constantly put you down and judged every move you made? Rather than throw my nasty roommate's butt out on the street, I would lean in closer to listen every time the jerk would talk and I would believe every word. Of course, in reality, the bully's voice was mine, but I felt powerless over it and listening to all those lies and judgements took me to a point where I couldn't take it anymore. Have you ever had that moment when you realize that the one person you're the most tired of being around is you?

I was caught in a pattern of trying to be happy while being my own worst critic. I finally hit the wall because I didn't want to face one more day of trying be funny when I was so miserable.

I didn't need anyone in the audience at those comedy clubs to criticize me or put me down because I was already doing a fine job at that myself. During one of the episodes of her long-running television show, Oprah Winfrey said, "*You are not your negative thoughts.*" Oprah was right (again!), because when you think about it, being a comedienne and a heckler all at the same time just doesn't make any sense.

One of those voices I was listening to wasn't real.

Or more accurately, one of those voices was not telling the truth.

You are not the negative thoughts in your head.

Your true nature is not negative at all.

Your true nature is not stress.

Your true nature is not worry.

Your true nature is not fear.

Your true nature is joy.

That's right. Joy. Big, bright, light-filled joy.

You subconsciously acknowledge your joyful true nature each time you are in a bad mood or stressed out and you say to someone, "*I'm sorry. I'm just not myself today.*"

To visualize your true nature, get out one of your baby photos or just think of a baby. Babies are bundles of pure love and light. Babies don't have "mind-chatter". When you were born, you didn't pop out and start thinking, "*Oh my god! What the hell just happened? That was a total disaster! And what's up with her? She looks like crap! Honey, brush your hair and put on some make-up for God's sake! Somebody call me a cab!*"

And because you had such a quiet mind, you were always happy and at peace with the world. Yes, babies cry and scream, but when they do it's purely for biological reasons. Those were the good ol' days, hey? Wouldn't it be great if the only time you got upset was when you were hungry, tired, or had just wet yourself?

I know we say that we love babies because they're so cute and they smell so good, but I think our love of babies runs deeper than their adorable looks and scented heads. I think we like having our true nature reflected back at us. We like being reminded of who we really are. Let's admit it, we cherish babies because it's awfully nice to spend time with humans who don't have any negative "mind-chatter" that puts them in a bad mood or causes them to dish out attitude. I really think I'm onto something here. If you are not convinced, just think about how all kinds of people talk about wanting to have a baby and no one ever talks about wanting to have a teenager.

So, guess what? I have good news to share. When it comes to being happy and at peace with the world, you had it nailed at the very beginning of your life. Yes, with your quiet mind and pure, uninterrupted focus on the present moment, you were already a little Zen master. There you were drooling away in your diapers happy and loving everyone and everything around you. There you were being bounced on someone's knee all the while exuding peacefulness, playfulness, curiosity, and enthusiasm. Funny enough, those states that we so easily embodied, and those behaviours we so effortlessly demonstrated, as a baby are the very things we are striving for when we pick up a self-help book, attend a yoga class, join a drum circle, sit in a therapy session, or walk on burning coals.

It may sound odd, but your "personal growth" process is actually done. It has always been done. It was done the day you arrived. The last time I checked, anything to do with "personal growth" is about being happier, more joyful, loving, peaceful, light-hearted, playful, and engaged with life. Doesn't that sound like how you were as a baby? Anything to do with "personal growth" describes the *real* you.

As we grow up we learn things like judgement and experiencing and expressing our joyful true nature becomes far more challenging. Some might even call it *work*.

Yes, it's challenging and yes it's work, but keep in mind that when it comes to seeing the lighter side of life, being happy, and being at peace with the world, there isn't anything to learn. Instead, there may very well be things to *un*-learn. As you were once a Zen master due to the absence of "mind-chatter", reclaiming your true nature involves *un*-learning the negative thought patterns and limiting beliefs that cause you to drift away from that joyful true nature of yours.

Your core, your truth, that light inside of you is always there – it's been there since the day you first showed up here. Think of your true nature as being ever-present like the sun. When you cannot see the sun during the day, it isn't because it ceases to exist, but rather, it's because your view of it is simply being blocked. The light is still there. When the clouds clear away or the fog lifts, you experience the light once again. Just like the sun, the way your true nature can be seen and experienced is by letting go of thinking that is blocking your light. Things like judgement, expectations, and the idea that there is not enough are these hindrances of the mind that much like clouds or fog, hinder our ability to see and be our true selves.

One of my favourite Zen proverbs states, "*Knowledge is learning something every day. Wisdom is letting go of something every day.*"

What have you learned along the way that has made it tough to be as peaceful and playful as you were when you first showed up here?

What do you need to let go of in order to be the *real* you?

It's not the letting go that hurts, but the holding on.

Fear just means you've become forgetful. You’ve forgotten how deeply you’re loved, how guided you are, and that brighter days will return, like you’ve never seen before.

Four

Seeing Nothing As Stress

"Every day brings a choice: to practice stress or to practice peace."

- Joan Borysenko

I was talking with a friend one early December and as we discussed our plans for the upcoming festive season, she informed me that she and her husband were not going to be visiting the in-laws that Christmas because they had decided to *avoid that stress.* I immediately asked her what their address was so I could avoid the area and have a shot at having happy holidays. Listening to my friend describe the plight that she was so excited to be avoiding, I couldn't help but visualize what could have the power to make her miserable. What had happened there in the past? Does stress hide in the front bushes and ambush her when she stands at the front door or maybe the in-laws put something funky in the dressing.

People talk about there being *so much stress at work* which creates another rather interesting image in my mind. I picture them arriving at work in the morning to a virtual land mine of distress. The stress is all over the floor, spilling out of the filing cabinets, and hanging from the fluorescents.

When I hear someone say, "*We've got that meeting today – that's going to bring on the stress*", I can't help but visualize someone sending Stress a meeting request through Microsoft Outlook and then Stress showing up at the boardroom decked out in a power suit ready to freak everyone right out.

My favourite expression is, "*I'm under stress.*" I don't know about you, but that just sounds downright kinky. Well, they say stress works for some people. Ahem.

Stress doesn't exist the way we often think and talk about it. There is a long-standing, collective belief that stress is an external circumstance, like the weather, and if and when, we find ourselves in its presence, our mindset automatically changes accordingly. The myth of stress is that we can encounter it like we can encounter a snow storm. It's not that we are delusional and have convinced ourselves that stress is some kind of invisible swamp thing that comes along and changes our state of mind, but I think our perception of stress makes many people believe that certain events, situations, and circumstances will inevitably make them want to run screaming and so they are considered forms of stress.

The myth of stress is disempowering. If we live with the belief that the freedom we desire comes from avoiding something or someone that controls how we feel and think (and therefore our stress levels), we are living an illusion that gives far too much power to our circumstances and not enough power to the perceptions and thoughts we create about our circumstances.

In his book, *The Happiness Advantage*, Shawn Achor, explains that based on findings from case study research, if he knew everything about your external circumstances, he would only be able to predict 10% of your long-term happiness. I'm certainly no mathematician, but I'm pretty sure that means 90% of your long-term happiness is determined by how your brain processes your external circumstances – which is just an analytical way of saying, "*where ever you go, there you are*".

Stress does exist, but think of the word, "stress" as a short form for *stressful thoughts*. You cannot experience stress without first creating (and believing) stressful thoughts. Stress is what you endure when you *perceive* your circumstances as stressful (perceived danger) and then that annoying "flaw in the system" kicks in because your body thinks you are facing real danger. In other words, it is actually your stressful thoughts that sets off the "false alarm."

It challenges a long-standing, collective idea, but the only realistic opportunity that you have to *avoid* stress is to *avoid* seeing and thinking about something in a stressful way.

The same concept applies to peace. People often talk about *finding peace,* which sounds like they set it down years ago and now can't for the life of them remember where they put it.

Throughout my childhood, my mother would often say, "*All I want is some peace and quiet.*" It was basically her mantra. Even though I was just a kid, I picked up on the impossible nature of my mother's request. I had never seen peace the way she was talking about it. Being a comedienne from a very early age, one Mother's Day I gave her a blank cassette tape and on the label I wrote, "PRESS PLAY FOR SOME PEACE AND QUIET". She played it over and over again.

Dr. Wayne Dyer once said, "*There is no way to peace. Peace is the way.",* because peace isn't something that is tucked away in one of the boxes in the garage. The only realistic way to *find peace* is to *find ways* to see and think about things that allows you to be peaceful. Or in other words, by choosing the lenses through which you view things.

There will be a day when you look back at all of this and shake your head and wonder why you worried so much. Skeptical? Think of all the times that has happened before.

The unplanned changes in your life are merely paths that appear that you didn't know you were meant to take.

Five

Seeing Nothing As Stressful

"...for there is nothing either good or bad, but thinking makes it so."

- Hamlet, William Shakespeare

Moving is stressful.

Starting a new job is stressful.

Planning a wedding is stressful.

The way we refer to things as being inherently stressful, it's as if events, situations, and circumstances come with tags attached to them indicating the appropriate response to have when you encounter them. Imagine if that was our reality. As you start packing up to change residences, you notice a message on one of your cardboard boxes that reads: "THIS IS STRESSFUL. START FREAKING OUT NOW." Or you visit www.whatisstressful.com

and you see that what you are dealing is indeed on the official list of things that cause stress which means you have no choice but to be stressed. Damn.

Those scenarios are not our reality, but at times, the way we think and talk about our external circumstances, it might as well be.

Along with the belief that stress is its own external circumstance (so avoid it if you can), another popular belief is that some external circumstances come to us containing a particular value and its value determines our mindset. But as Hamlet expressed to Rosencrantz and Guildenstern, nothing comes to us containing a value. For something to be stressful, it requires judgement – you must see it and think about it as stressful.

Good ol' Shakespeare nailed the truth (as he so often did)–everything and everyone around us is completely neutral. The neutrality of everything is what you observe before it goes through your "filter" where you give it meaning and add your interpretation. The neutrality of everything is often a challenging concept to comprehend because the facts go through our "filter" so quickly and that rapid process tricks us into thinking that our judgement is the truth. Because we form judgements so often, we rarely see things for what they are. The world around us doesn't get to speak for itself and even if it could, it wouldn't be able to get a word in edgewise because we're too busy giving everything meaning and interpreting it in some way.

The meaning we give something, and our interpretation of it (our "judgement"), creates a story in our mind. Our stories are basically judgements that we assume to be 100% truth. As life unfolds, we tell ourselves so many stories about the things that we encounter and one of those stories is that something is *stressful*. Something being stressful of its own accord is a story because there are no tags or official list indicating the value of anything.

We tell ourselves all kinds of stories because we want to give everything meaning. Everything that does, and does not, occur means something to us. When we win, when we lose, when we mess up, when someone dislikes us, when we struggle, when we shine, when we forget to do something really important – it all means something and then we convince ourselves that that meaning (which is completely made up) is fact and that "imagined truth" takes our freedom of choice away. When we view something as stressful, that gives us only one option for how we will experience it. *Are you kidding me? I can't possibly be calm during such a stressful time.*

When we see everything as neutral, we open ourselves up to experiencing something the way we want to, rather than operating from some kind of default position.

Seek freedom by choosing to see things exactly as they are.

When my friend (and fellow seeker) Kelly Elson and I were discussing the neutrality of everything one day, she used an analogy – everything is like water. By adding or subtracting heat, water can be transformed into a different state – slush, snow, ice, steam, vapour, etc. Much like choosing a certain temperature, the lenses we select alter everything we observe and that shapes how we experience it. Just like adjusting temperature can transform the state of water, adjusting our perception can transform the state of what we observe and experience.

We may say, "*This is such a stressful week.*" However, the truth is that it is a week. Again, there is no label on the calendar stating this and no pre-warning to book a vacation. That week may contain certain events, appointments and scheduled tasks; however, the "stressful" part is entirely due to perception. It can only be a stressful week if you see it and think about it in that way.

Even though you may think, "*I work with some stressful people*", no one has actually ever come up to you at work with a tag hanging from their arm that says, "I AM HERE TO MERELY PISS YOU OFF." No, not even *that* person!
Sure, there are changes and challenges in life that dare us to give up and start drinking gin and tonic at

breakfast, but that's the point – life only delivers us neutral circumstances such as people, weeks, changes, and challenges. The rest of the "story" is determined by how you look at them.

I'm not suggesting that stressful things don't exist. In fact, it's quite possible that you're dealing with something stressful right now. What I am suggesting is that the reason something appears stressful is entirely due to perception. Because everything is neutral, like water, something being stressful is only due to your state of mind and your perception that it is stressful. Just like you can experience water in many ways, the world around us can be stressful or peaceful (or something entirely different) depending on how you look at it. Life contains many change and challenges, but whether it is good, bad, peaceful, stressful, or something else, is entirely up to you and your perception.

Have you ever noticed that everything is made up? And I'm not just talking about the things you can see. I'm talking about everything. Thoughts, belief systems, and the stories you play over and over again in your mind. The ideas of "right" and "wrong". What is "good" and "bad". That being selfish is a sin, being rich is evil, or being sexy is vulgar. All made up. It's every man for himself. Made up. No pain, no gain. Made up. Better safe than sorry. It's all made up! Challenge everything that you tell yourself and the world tells you because you can. And then decide what is true for you. And if you've never done this before, don't worry, just make it up as you go along.

The best way to tell if something is meant to be is to trust that everything is.

Six

The Female Brain Versus The Male Brain (Why We Stress About The Stuff That We Do And Why The Reasons Are Different)

Have you ever noticed that men and women get stressed about totally different things? While a woman paces around the living room going on about something someone said to her at work, her husband's only concern is that she's blocking the TV when the big game is on.

Stereotypical? Yes. Biological reasons that explain that common scenario? Yes.

As I was preparing to speak at an International Women's Day event at a college, I not-so-randomly stumbled upon the work of Dr. K.A. Pradeep who wrote a book called, *The Buyer's Brain*. In the book, he explains how to market to males and females based on the different designs and functions of their brains. As it turns out, our brains are designed based on the different roles we had back at the very beginning of human civilization. As cavemen and cavewomen we performed very different tasks in contrasting environments and as a result modern men and women are hardwired to stress out about different things. There are also scientific and biological reasons why we are so different in the way we access our power, find our strength, and feel the most at ease.

If you're a woman reading this, would you say that you get stressed when you are busy? And would you say that is a significant challenge because well, you seem to be busy most of the time? If those last two questions don't apply to you for whatever reason (and that reason may be that you are male), are there busy women around you who talk about being stressed because they're so busy?

Chances are one of those questions rang true for you because women are hard-wired to be busy. Women's brains are designed to multi-task. Keep in mind that the design of the female brain was influenced by the cavewoman lifestyle. Back in the very beginning, the cavewoman's days were multi-focused. While the men were off hunting all day, the women were back at the cave keeping the home fires burning, supporting each other, gathering nuts and berries, and taking care of the children. Because of the various tasks the females were involved in, they used and developed both the left and right hemispheres of their brains. And that is precisely why most women tend to be busy, feel guilty or unworthy when they are not busy, love talking about being busy (*Show-off*), or praise other people for being busy and then secretly wonder why they can't be as busy as them.

It may be thousands of years later, but women still have brains that are designed based on their cavewoman roots. Here in the twenty-first century, women still have many more connections between their right and left hemispheres than a typical male. The female brain is hardwired to juggle tasks, emotions, information, and to-do lists.

So there it is. Females are designed and therefore destined to be busy. May we women accept that we're hardwired that way rather than wishing we were leading different lives. The fact of the matter is, if we ran off to Italy to live a simple life in Tuscany, we would probably end up owning and operating our own winery while renovating our villa and writing all about it in our blog that we plan to turn into a book later.

There is also a reason why women like being together any chance they get. While the men were off hunting, the women were living in a community, supporting each other, caring for their children, and doing whatever else was needed to help each other keep the home fires burning. Based on this collective lifestyle, female brains are community-oriented.

Female brains are designed to be social, to nurture and to protect. Women are hardwired for networking, efficiency, and empathy. The top achievement for females was (and still is) connection. It is because of this reliance on each other way back at the beginning that modern woman feels the strongest and most comfortable when she has a sense of belonging.

So what about the male brain? What does it seek? In the caveman days, men spent most of their time off hunting. Their one and only job was to go out and kill a wild animal and bring it home to the family for dinner. Because cavemen had the role of being a provider, male brains are goal-oriented. Men are hardwired to acquire and achieve. The male brain seeks reward and pleasure.

While the cavewomen thrived in their network, the cavemen lifestyle was solitary. The men would go out hunting with the incentive to be "that guy" – the one who brought back the biggest and best carcass. Because of the male's desire to be "that guy", the top achievement for men was independence. They didn't want the help from others. Now you know there is a neurological reason why men don't want to stop and ask for directions.

These differences between the male and female brains are reflected in many ways in our modern world because our psyches haven't changed despite our dramatically different lifestyles and environments.

Current statistics indicate that men speak an average of 7,000 words a day while women speak an average of 22,000 words a day. Independence versus community. Man Cave versus Book Club (also known as a good excuse to drink wine)...and Pampered Chef parties, coffee dates, lunch dates, girls night out, spa days, clothing swaps, yoga retreats, and the list goes on.

In light of the differences between the design and the function of the female brain and the male brains, what tends to stress out women and men is (most likely not shockingly) different as well.

Here are the three major differences between the sexes when it comes to stress:

1. The female brain remembers stressful and negative experiences more than the male brain does. That explains why women remember everything that was said during an argument that happened ten years ago and men have no recollection of the argument even taking place.

2. The female brain views life events as potentially catastrophic. Women tend to make things bigger, uglier, scarier, and far more life-threatening than they really are. While it usually takes the threat of immediate physical danger for men to reach a high level of agitation.

These two differences in men and women are readily apparent in the following modern day conversation. Woman says to man: "*I can't believe you don't remember what she said to me! That night was a huge disaster! I'll never recover from that!*" Man responds to woman: "*Ah, get over it. No one died!*"

The female knack for remembering conflicts, giving them a great deal of meaning, and interpreting them in ways that make them appear catastrophic makes perfect sense considering that back in the very beginning, conflict with other women in the community could sever the chain of support and put your life in danger. Harmony in the community served basic, primal needs. Without the support of other women in the community, a woman's survival and the survival of her children was greatly threatened. Because of the strong reliance on other women for health and safety, the biggest threat (and therefore the biggest fear) was ostracism.

Same brain, just thousands of years later. With these roots deeply embedded within the female psyche, women today elevate conflicts, disagreements, and other forms of social tension to life-threatening emergency status. Women are essentially hardwired to afflict themselves with that perceived danger and respond to things in ways that create the same intense feelings associated with facing real danger. If you are a woman, a good way to tell when you're caught up catastrophic thinking is to notice those times when you are thinking about something and your eyes get really big and shifty, like one of those soap opera characters having a dramatic flash back. As you intently listen to and believe the story playing out in your mind, you look like you're remembering that time when you were kidnapped by your hostile ex-lover and held captive for several months.

3. The female brain is hard-wired to plan for the future far more than the male brain. Back in the very beginning, the cavewoman's fixation on the future was rather primal – her concerns were related to survival. The unknown future involved the threat of real danger so her worries were related to the potential amount of food and protection that would be available. Cavewomen had to stay a step ahead if they were going to survive and this meant constantly arranging for food and shelter.

Same brain, just thousands of years later. Those roots run deep within the female psyche. Here in the twenty-first century, that primal fixation on the future and its potential real danger has evolved into perceived danger (stressful thoughts) about what to wear to a dinner party, whether or not the presentation will go well, or if the kids will get to swim practice on time tomorrow. Now you know why women start talking about Christmas in the middle of the summer and why men don't start their Christmas shopping until December 24th.The good ol' "what if's". Because we're so busy, I suppose it's handy that we get so much of our worrying done ahead of time.

If you are a woman, a good way to lighten up is to know that you come by your stress honestly rather than wishing that you were different.

Because you most likely are busy, make sure you are busy doing things that lift you up and give yourself permission to relax and play.

Because you most likely are constantly planning for the future, see if you can consciously set aside time to do that planning rather than let those thoughts constantly pull you away from being in the moment.

Because you most likely fret about the future, notice when you start worrying about the unknown and decide to be at peace with not knowing.

Because you most likely give social conflict meaning and interpret it in a dramatic way, let go of all that catastrophic thinking and focus on the truth. The truth is, you're not a cavewoman and no matter what happened or what she said, you will survive.

If you are a man, just stay safe.

There is a direct link between how you view yourself and how you view the world. The more you choose to love yourself unconditionally, the more you realize and accept that you don't need anyone's approval and you care less about what other people think of you.

“It’s not what you look at that matters, it’s what you see.”

- Henry David Thoreau

Seven

Noticing How Good You've Got It

"Everything is amazing and we're still not happy."

- Louis C.K.

Have you ever noticed the horror on some people's faces when their cell phone signal drops in the middle of their conversation? Somehow it's shockingly easy to experience an intense state of despair and frustration while holding a phone that used to be attached to our kitchen wall. Not only are we holding the kitchen phone in our hands, but nowadays most of us are holding the computer as well. The "smart phone" is a revolutionary piece of technology, but we'll be damned if it's slow connecting us to the Internet. Sure, it's an outstanding time in history as we hold a device in our hands that magically sends and receives signals to and from Mars, but if it takes a few extra seconds to do that, it's deemed a piece of crap and we want a new one.

The fact that so much stress exists in this extremely affluent era is what I call "the paradox of prosperity". Even though our standard of living has steadily risen over the last several decades, our sense of personal satisfaction has not budged. We are no happier than when we had to churn our own butter.

Here are some other signs of this "paradox of prosperity":

- You want to show your friend this hilarious video you found on YouTube and you start freaking out because the link no longer works.

- You lose it when you realize you can't watch a TV show because you are already PVRing two other channels (and you don't have one of those fancy new PVRs that have solved that so-called "dilemma").

- You march right back into Starbucks and give that barista a piece of your mind after realizing that she put 2% milk instead of skim milk in your latte *and* it isn't extra hot.

- You want to throw your iPad clear across the room because when you hold it vertically the image on the screen goes horizontal and then when you hold it horizontally the image on the screen goes vertical (and repeat).

- You can't get the Wi-Fi password to work and you kind of don't know how to go on in life.

- You are furious that you have to sit in the middle seat on your flight *and* the fact that the plane doesn't have those small, individual screens triggers a tiny meltdown.

- After you accidentally dial someone on your car's Bluetooth system, you begin cursing while frantically (and randomly) pressing all the buttons on your steering wheel.

- You drop the F-bomb each and every time that rainbow wheel (or hourglass, for you PC users) appears on your computer screen.

- Your reaction to the Internet being down is not far off from how you'd react if you were suddenly stranded on a deserted island.

Despite this era of affluence, with its unprecedented choice of goods and services and a staggering amount of access to them, we still manage to focus on there not being enough. The examples listed above illustrate that despite all the advancements in technology and gadgets, we still want more, faster, and better.

The reason this "paradox of prosperity" exists is because the concepts of "enough" and "lack" are both perceptions. Our sense of personal satisfaction hasn't elevated along with our standard of living because when we think there isn't enough, there never will be.

Challenge your stories about there being lack in your life and focus on the truth. The truth is you have always had enough. I probably don't know you personally, but I do know that you have always had enough because you are reading this book right now. You have made it this far which proves that you have always had everything you have ever needed to make it to this very moment.

Gratitude turns what you have into enough.

What can heal your thoughts about there not being enough and shift your focus away from the things that are missing? You can practice seeing how good you've got it, how much you do have and how many things truly are going well. Make a deliberate choice to see the abundance around you.

Abundance isn't something you acquire in this life, but rather, it is something you are aware of.

The next time life dares you to complain or you find yourself stressed out because you're focusing on what's missing, choose an "attitude of gratitude". I know it sounds totally cheesy, but it rhymes and when something rhymes, it tends to stick. You don't ever have to say it, but consider doing it because stress cannot exist where there is gratitude.

For example, when you're stuck in a traffic jam, rather than get all stressed out and irritated, tune into the abundance. Sit back in your driver's seat and notice how fortunate you are to be dealing with this traffic jam in the first place. Wow, look at you and your car. Cars are expensive and no matter how slow the traffic is, walking would take much longer. You're still ahead.

The next time you're standing in a long checkout line at the grocery store, rather than get all frustrated and impatient, tune into the abundance. There you are standing with a cart full of groceries. Notice how fortunate you are to be in a place with all kinds of foods and products readily available and the biggest issue right now is that you have to wait for a few minutes to buy all that stuff in your cart with your money. Wow, look at you in a grocery store. And by the way, no matter how long the checkout line is, I'm pretty sure hunting and gathering all that food would take longer. Again, you're still ahead, baby. #firstworldproblems

In *The Book of Awesome*, author Neil Pasricha focuses on being aware and grateful for the small pleasures in life such as the smell of freshly cut grass, that very first sip of coffee in the morning, and that cool feeling on your face when you flip your pillow over to the other side.

I, for one, am grateful that spiders don't fly. That's awesome.

Rather than curse and growl when Facebook is taking forever to upload on to your phone, notice the rather awesome thing that your phone is doing. Wow, look at you walking around with your kitchen phone and a computer in your hand! As you tune in to the abundance and the gratitude sets in, you'll find yourself delighted by the small wonders of life. "*Wow! Someone I hardly even know wants to be my friend!*"

The next time you're sitting in traffic, remember me, won't you? Rather than focusing on there not being enough time for this or there not being enough lanes on the highway, tune into the abundance. Just sit back and say, "*Wow! Look at me in my car!*" And if the guy in the lane beside you looks all stressed out, look over at him and smile. Lower your window and yell out, "*Wow! Look at you in your car!*" Now, you're likely going to get the finger, but you'll be fine because stress does not exist where there is gratitude.

It has been proven that people who practice gratitude are far less likely to experience depression and anxiety. It isn't that people are grateful because their happy, it's that people are happy because they're grateful.

In these busy times when you are battling with pieces of technology that only work some days, practice gratitude by noticing how good you've got it, how much you do have and how many things are going well. It has helped me lighten up many times. No matter how long it has taken me to drive somewhere, I can't help but smile each and every time my GPS tells me that I have arrived.

During the tough times, people often say, "*This too shall pass.*" This is true. However, what we tend to forget is that same truth also applies to the good times.

Loving yourself unconditionally is so important if you want to be truly happy and at peace with the world. If there's one thing I know, it's that negative self-talk sure can make you bitchy.

Eight

Put Down Your Crystal Ball

I was out running once and ahead of me in the near distance was a group of teenage boys. What do you call that by the way? A gaggle? A herd? Let's go with herd. As I ran toward the herd of teenage boys, I suddenly realized that in a few moments, I would be running around them and then I would be running directly in front of them displaying my rear end in my rather form-fitting running shorts. You know that feeling of dread because you know exactly what is going to happen? Yes, I had that feeling because I had my crystal ball out and I knew how those teenage boys were going to react as I was running in front of them.

Anytime we refer to the future with any amount of certainty, we are caught up in a story because it hasn't happened yet. These stories we tell ourselves or other people about the future is kind of a twisted form of "fortune telling". Yes, we haul around our crystal balls telling ourselves and the people around us about the impending chaos, misfortune, and hardship we are going to face. "*This is going to be a total disaster.*" "*That will end up to be a complete waste of time.*" "*She is going to freak right out when she hears this.*" The professionals are really good at only telling us positive things while we amateurs seems to have a real knack for solely spreading the doom and gloom. May we never quit our day jobs and go into the business of telling people their futures because no one would ever come back to us for another session because they would be spending that money on therapy.

Now, back to my story...As I drew nearer to what I believed was my fate, I started preparing myself for the derogatory remarks. I began gearing up for the sexist comments. I could already hear their catcalls (if I was lucky!). Any small amount of joy I received from running was completely gone because I was believing these negative thoughts that were not true. They were not true because they were about something that hadn't even happened yet. That's the thing about fear – we never fear what is, we always fear what isn't. So there I was running around downtown Toronto carrying my big, crystal ball which was quite a good workout – great for the core.

The stories we tell about the future (fortune telling), are not only a source of stress, but they are examples of limited thinking. When you talk about the future with any amount of certainty, it's like looking out at the countless possibilities that lay before you and narrowing it down to one option, and only one option. And chances are it ain't pretty.

The monumental moment arrived and I held my breath as I ran around the boys and then ran in front of them leaving them with a clear view of my rear end. At first there was silence and then all of a sudden, one of the boys from the group yelled out at the top of his lungs, "I believe in you!" A few moments later they all cheered me on. That was it! The experience of jogging in front of those teenage boys was not only very different than what I had predicted, it was downright inspiring.

How many times have you known exactly how something is going to be, like I knew how it was going to be running in front of those teenage boys? And how many times has life surprised you, like those teenage boys surprised me that day? How many times has the future turned out to be different (and a hell of a lot better) than you thought it would be? That experience with those boys reminded me how powerful it can be to challenge the stories we create about the future.

When you get out your crystal ball (and trust me, you will) catch yourself in the act and then remind yourself that because you don't know what is going to happen, anything is possible. One way to lighten up is to notice how much you don't know about the future and fearlessly choose to live in the mystery.

When a door in your life just won't open, it's only because there's more to gain by staying where you are.

Got any patterns in your life? Those are just lessons that keep coming around and they will keep coming around until you learn them. The Universe totally believes in 17th chances.

Nine

How To Cure A Case Of The "Shoulds"

"When the resistance is gone, so are the demons."

- Pema Chödrön

Have you ever noticed how tough it is to accept something just as it is?

When the weather is cold, we crank up the heat…and complain about winter.

When the weather is hot, we sit in air conditioning… and complain about the humidity.

When we get older, we buy anti-aging products and colour our hair.

When we gain weight, we try to lose it.

When we're alone, we want company.

When we're surrounded by many people, we yearn for solitude.

When it's noisy, we want silence.

When there is silence, we feel it's too quiet.

We even dress dead people up to like they're alive and well...and headed to a cocktail party.

For some reason, we're addicted to wanting things to be different than they are which wouldn't matter much if that resistance didn't result in stress. Think of something that is stressing you out right now and I bet that at the very source of your struggle lies a wish to change someone or something that you cannot change. Whatever it is, just consider what it would feel like to stop arguing with reality and accept that person (who might be yourself) or accept that circumstance. What would it feel like it to be at one with it rather than against it? Acceptance prevents you from expending your precious energy and experiencing the stress that comes along with trying to change people or circumstances in your life that cannot be changed.

It may sound like I'm suggesting that a good way to lighten up about stuff is to roll over and play dead or stop caring, but that's not it at all. Acceptance sounds passive, but consider the power it gives you to finally embrace reality. Until you decide to be at one with something, you can't go forward and get through it.

When you think about acceptance this way, it isn't passive at all; it's actually a very progressive and active process. If you don't first hold something, however can you heal it? If you're busy resisting your reality, how can you come up with an idea, decision, or solution to get past it? How can you move forward if you're stuck there with your arms crossed saying to yourself, "*I can't believe this is happening.*"?

When I began my Human Resources career, I spent the first several months wishing my life was different. The stress that I experienced from being in a constant state of resistance led me to decide to quit. Keep in mind that my previous job was as a stand-up comic. I didn't exactly understand how things worked in the "real world" and I had no idea that there may be some paperwork and a process to resigning from a job. No, I just stood up at my desk, walked over to my manager's office and told her that I was leaving. Nancy, my manager (God bless her), smiled at me and asked me to go home that evening and think about it before making my final decision.

As I sat at home contemplating my next move, I realized that I didn't have another plan. I had absolutely no idea what I would do next. Facing the daunting prospect of playing in the traffic for what could end up to be weeks, months, or possibly years, I decided to stay.

The moment I decided to stay I made a vow to stop fighting the direction of my path and accepted it. I stopped grasping for something else (that wasn't there, by the way) and let go. I simply let things be.

This action of non-action is often referred to as, "surrender" because metaphorically speaking, you are putting down the weapons and giving up the fight to control things. To surrender means not asking, "*How can this be happening?*" or "*Why is this happening?*", but asking, "*What will I make of it?*"

I was still at a complete loss as to how this dramatic change in my vocation was going to make sense in my life at all, but I made a commitment to stop wishing things were different and be at one with it all. I decided to see the present moment as my friend, rather than my enemy. Not only did I enter a state of acceptance, but I vowed to view it as the adventure it truly was and have as much fun with it as possible. When I finally decided to hold it, I was able to heal it.

I went back to work the next day, poked my head into Nancy's office and said, "*Hi Nancy. Just kidding!*"

I stayed at the Human Resources department in the Ontario Government for the next five years. In my state of surrender, I brought my spirit and personality to my work. Before long I was using my skills as a stand-up comic to host awards ceremonies and create my first inspirational presentation.

I have come to realize that the best way to take care of the future is to embrace the present.

When you find yourself arguing with some aspect of your reality, surrender to your path – especially on those days when you wish your life came with background music so you could understand what the hell is going on.

What has helped me to be more accepting is to understand what causes the resistance in the first place. When we want someone to be different than they are or something to be different than it is, it's because we have shown up with expectations. Expectations are the images we create in our mind about how something is going to be, look, or feel. Perhaps even riskier, these images are of how people are going to be, respond, or behave. When we show up to something or someone in our life with an expectation and life doesn't match that expectation, we resist and argue with reality. I think of expectations as resentments in waiting and stress under construction.

There is a little trick that can help you notice when you're caught up in an expectation. Anytime you're stuck in an expectation, you think or say the word, "should".

Have you ever had a bad case of the "shoulds"?

This should not be happening.

Things around here should be a lot different.

He should know better by now.

She should apologize to her.

I should get out more.

They should not be getting married.

We should not have to be dealing with any of this.

He should find a good therapist.

She should mind her own business…and I should tell her!

It sure is tough to see the lighter side of life when you're standing there should-ing yourself.

As I sat there in my cubicle wishing things in my life matched the image I had created in my mind, I remember thinking to myself, I should still be doing stand-up comedy. I should not be working in a Human Resources department in the Ontario Government.

Next time you see someone stressed out because they're wanting something to be different than it is or someone to be different than they are, go ahead and help them to see what's causing their struggle. Go for it. Go up to them and say, "Hey, enough of your expectations. You're should-ing all over the place!"

The shoulds are like an imaginary law book that we carry around that tells us how we and everyone else are supposed to be doing things. The truth is, besides what's in the real law books (seriously, you should not kill someone), everything else is optional.

Consider that the time in your life when you were the most at peace and happiest was also the time in your life before you learned to have expectations. Show me a nine or ten month old baby crawling around all stressed out because it's thinking, "I should be walking by now!"

Remember when you were a kid and you couldn't wait to grow up? You couldn't wait to get older because then you could do whatever you want whenever you want! How's that working out with all those expectations you're now trying to live up to?

I want to do this. But I should do that.

But first I want to take a nap. But I should do it now.

The way to cure a case of the shoulds is to challenge what you think the world expects of you.

I know, I know, you and I and everybody else have been fed so many rules and standards to live up to, but there is freedom in realizing that all those rules are completely made-up. Those rules and standards are just collective opinions based on conditioning.

Despite what we may think, we can do anything we want. We don't have to do anything we don't want to. Yes, there are always consequences to consider, but the truth is we can do whatever we want. We can have all the adventures we want and learn all the hard life lessons we want. We can fumble and bumble around just as much as the next person. We can trip up, fall down, fall short, and marry the wrong person.

In fact, not only can we do whatever we want, the Universe is cheering us on because we're doing what we set out to do – evolve through the human experience. We are all here on sacred journeys. Whether you want to call it dharma or destiny, we are all living out our own unique set of adventures and learning a specific set of lessons, all in the name of evolution. Whatever we face in our lives has been lovingly sent in order for us to take that next step along our path. Here's the irony.... the key to accepting everyone and everything is living with the knowledge that everything is exactly as it should be.

Want to be happy? Live your truth and speak your truth. Always be authentic. Except for when your doctor asks you how many drinks you have per week. Make something up.

If something different was supposed to be happening, than something different would be happening. Trust the path.

Ten

Accepting The “Flux Of Life”: Seeing The Lighter Side Of Change

“As any good Buddhist will tell you, the only way to find permanent joy is by embracing the fact that nothing is permanent.”

- Martha Beck

We push away change as often as Kanye West pushes away members of the paparazzi. The fact that we resist change is actually the reason why we get so stressed when it comes along. As I have learned the hard way through much experience, anytime there is stress, someone is arguing with their reality. Go ahead and put that to the test. Think of something that you’re stressing about right now and I guarantee you that it is because you are resisting something. I guarantee that you want someone to be different than they are or you want something to be different than it is. All stress is created by saying “no” to your current life experience in some way.

Now we may not want to admit to this truth, but we have a hard time accepting change because we *expect* things to last. With our expectation that things will last, we view change as something that comes along and disrupts the flow of life.

Our expectation that things will last sets us up for a constant struggle with change because here in the physical world, impermanence is the rule. Nothing stays static. No living thing, no organization, no circumstance, and no relationship stays the same.

And yet, despite all the impermanence around us, we expect to one day get the ground under our feet. Isn't it adorable how we expect things to finally calm down one day? Bless our hearts for expecting things to quiet down so that we'll get everything sorted out once and for all. Here we are trying to gain this sense of comfort from having everything in place when the reality is, things come together and they fall apart. Things come together again and they fall apart again. Things come together again and they fall apart again. And repeat. We strive to feel settled in a world where nothing really ever gets solved. Everything and everyone is a work in progress. The truth is that everything and everyone is continuously evolving – our journey is a never-ending one. For example, right now it's 2014 and they are still improving the toothbrush.

Look around and you can see evidence of impermanence everywhere. The passage of time, the earth's rotation around the sun, the phases of the moon, and the ocean's currents are all examples of "flux" – the constant shifting, moving, and evolving that we see unfolding all around us.

Anything that is not changing is not living. The "flux" that occurs in your life is an indication that you're still breathing.

With all this change around us, it's rather fascinating that we're so shocked when it happens in our lives. Our reaction to change reminds me of the reaction we, Canadians, have to winter. Even though we know that winter is an inevitable aspect of our climate, when the first snowfall of the season arrives, we stand at our windows in amazement. "*Oh my God, it's snowing! Come over here! You gotta see this!*" Cue the mad, last minute scramble for snow shovels, snow blowers, snow tires, and non-freezing windshield washer fluid. And somehow we forget how to drive in the snow, even though it comes every year.

Rather than asking, "*Will change happen?*", ask, "*When will change happen?*"

Yes, change is also a gift. If it weren't for "flux", we would still be churning our own butter. We can thank "flux" for all the advancements that have ever taken place in modern civilization. And thanks to the "flux" in your life, you have advanced in your journey. You know who you know, you know what you know, and you can do what you do all because of "flux".

Seeing change as an expression of this physical law of "flux" (kind of like gravity) is where acceptance can begin because it is our expectation that things will remain the same that creates resistance.

To help you get comfy with idea that everything must change (and so it will), notice that it's always been like that and that you're already kind of a pro at riding the wave...

Your ship came in (at last!) and then you were lost at sea...without a paddle.

You were thin and then you weren't...or the other way around. (You own a few sizes of pants too, hey?)

You had lots of money. And then you didn't. And then you had lots of money again. (Repeat.)

You saw things as black and white and now you're all about the shades of grey.

You were BFFs...for a while.

You were overwhelmed and scared. And now you can do it with your eyes shut. ("flux" can be quite liberating too!)

You rented for what seemed like an eternity and then the day came when you finally got a piece of the pie. Now you rent again.

You had great hair and then your hair stylist moved far away and you've never quite gotten your lid back to looking that good.

You were in love. And then you were alone. And now you're in love again. For now...

You were large and in charge. And then you were de-throned.

You had a booming business or career. And then you didn't. And then you reinvented yourself. And now it's the slow, steady build back up.

You were hip, you were cool, you were happening. And then one day you found yourself watching The Grammy Awards and you could barely identify any band or artist that appeared on the screen.

And now you feel really old at the mall. You have no business going into stores like "Forever 21" and you yearn for a store called, "Forever 39" where you can buy wine and yoga pants all in the same place.

Rather than seeing change as something disrupting the flow of life, see that it *is* the flow of life. You are experiencing the "flux of life" because you are part of this physical world that is constantly shifting, moving, and evolving. You're riding the wave, baby, which means you are alive! Anything that is living is changing. Next time you wish things would stay the same, consider the alternative. Ahem.

The next time change occurs in your life, imagine how good it will feel to embrace it with open arms. Imagine how good it will feel when you stare down change and simply say, "*Ah flux*".

The cool thing about things falling apart is that you get to choose the pieces you want to pick up.

Accepting yourself is so important – especially when you see yourself in photos because that moment can be quite a reality check sometimes. I realize I have “reverse anorexia” – I think I'm thinner than I actually am.

Eleven

Exercise (bear with me…this will be quick and relatively pain-free, I promise)

Remember the mind-body connection? It's a two-way street. Just like the mind can influence the state of the body, the body can influence the state of your mind. This connection still has everything to do with chemicals, but the difference is that your mind is the one being changed. When you get that heart of yours pumping and get your body all sweaty by doing some form of exercise, those lovely endorphins get released and they produce that oh-so beloved calm feeling known as the "relaxation response". That chilled out feeling you get during and after exercise is the effect of the "relaxation response". When that physiological change happens (the rise in your endorphin level), a change in your outlook follows. When you feel more relaxed and calm after exercising, don't you find that things look different? Not literally, of course, but don't you find that your perception changes? An issue doesn't seems so complex, a challenge doesn't seem so daunting, or you're not worried as much as you were about something. The actual circumstance hasn't changed, but how you're looking at and thinking about it has.

God bless exercise. Not only can it help you maintain a positive mindset, but when you start taking everything too seriously, it can peel you off the ceiling in no time. All that and you can avoid walking around wearing a "sugar tire" or looking like a "bird bath".

Because the mind-body connection is a two-way street, I try to exercise as much as possible. Every morning I do five sit-ups. I know it doesn't sound like much, but there are only so many times you can hit the snooze button.

Just like anything, exercise is most effective when you make it a habit. To make exercise a habit, do something for at least 20 minutes several times a week. Pick an activity that you like to do – something that will get your heart pumping and body all sweaty. If your mind just went into the gutter, that's fine, and just for the record, that activity does count. Just keep in mind that you are going to have to convince the other person to do it for at least 20 minutes several times a week. You might just want to consider power-walking instead.

If you already do exercise regularly, my advice is to keep it to yourself. Let's admit it, unless you fell off the treadmill and smacked your face, no one wants to hear about your workout. I just love these running "apps" people put on their iPhones that track the exact distance they run and then that important information becomes their latest Facebook status. You can only see that stuff come up in your newsfeed so often until you start thinking it might be time to "unfriend". Nobody wants to see that someone just ran another 10 km in record time while you're drinking a cocktail and eating some Pringles. No thank you.

If you have no plans to exercise in this lifetime, then keep in mind that your breathing, facial expression, and physical posture can positively influence your outlook. It's true that those three things are a result of your outlook, but just like the mind-body connection, it works both ways. Slow, deep breaths, smiling, and relaxed shoulders are all physical changes that release those good feeling chemicals into your bloodstream that are normally quite expensive and highly illegal.

Try this.

Stand up. Hold this book in your right hand. Put all your weight on your right foot and place your left foot on your right calf. Now stand up tall. Smile. Shoulders relaxed. Breathe deeply. Nice slow, even inhales and exhales. Now raise your arms up to the sky. Are you shoulders still nice and relaxed? Ok, good. Now, it might be hard to read along right now, but we're almost done. Are you still smiling and breathing deeply? Great. So now you're doing what is typically called, "Tree Pose" in yoga. Feel better? I thought so. And guess what, I just tricked you into exercising too. Yes, I'm that good. You're welcome.

"Fortunately, disappointments have little to do with circumstance and everything to do with perspective."

- Mike Dooley

How you feel in the present is largely determined by how you feel about your past. How you view things and think about the present largely determines your future.

Twelve

Be Here Now

I'm about to sing the praises of placing your attention on the present moment. Personally, I find this particular part of the "work" very challenging. If I'm not "on my game", my mind can easily drift to the past and the future hundreds of times throughout one day. Someone will start talking to me and, at first, I'm right there with them and then a few moments later, my eyes glaze over. As they continue to talk to me, I can hear sounds and I can see their mouth moving, but at that point, I'm debating whether I remembered to turn on the dishwasher before I left my house that morning.

The mind naturally wants to wander – we (women more than men) are actually hardwired to replay the past and fret about the future. The challenge of our mind doing all this wandering away from the present moment is that it impacts how we feel. When we are depressed or down, it's because we are thinking of something in our past and anytime we are anxious, it's because we are focused on the future. All our stressful thoughts are related to what has happened or may happen which is what makes the practice of being present so powerful.

Let's put that last statement the test. Think of something that you are stressed about. (I apologize that I am doing this again – it will be quick, I promise!). I guarantee you that whatever is stressing you out relates to something that has happened in your past or may happen in your future.

I once proclaimed this "rule" about stress (that it's always connected to the past or future) in a talk I was giving and a lady in the audience said, "*That isn't true. I'm stressed about the construction happening on my street right now.*" I told her that I wasn't aware that I was giving a talk in the middle of her street.

The key part of this "rule" is that anytime we are feeling good it is because our attention is on the present moment. Any time your focus is on the here and the now, your stories fade away and all that "mind-chatter" turns to stillness. When your mind is quiet, you can't help but see the lighter side of life because there are no thoughts that suggest otherwise.

The practice of being in the present moment is the act of meditation. You can actually be meditating anywhere you are. I took a course on the traditional practice of meditation referred to as "sitting", which is the act of sitting quietly in a comfortable position focusing only on your breath. As I learned in the course, anytime you find yourself caught up in a story about the past or future, just take that as a signal to let go of that story and begin again. To begin again in a "sitting" meditation means to return to the breath. In life, it means to return to the present moment. If you need to "let go" and "begin again" one hundred and eighty times in a day (like I do!), so be it.

If you're not into traditional meditation, here are three other ways you can practice being in the present moment in your life...

Be In The Car

When you are driving your car, check and see if you are in the car. I know that you will be physically in your car, but where will your attention be? Are you replaying a recent conversation you had with your mother? Are you reeling from what happened in that meeting? Do you have your crystal ball out telling yourself how that person is going to react to your news? How many times have you been caught up in stories of the past and future all while operating a heavy piece of machinery at high speed? There have been so many times that I have pulled into my driveway, parked my car, sat back, and thought to myself, "Now, how the hell did I get here? I hope everybody is ok!"

Be In The Shower

When you are in the shower in the morning, check and see if you are in the shower. How many times do you stand there and you're already in the middle of your busy day. As you're standing there in the shower, naked and dripping wet, are you writing that email, having that conversation, or doing something on your to-do list? Consider how many times you have showered with the people you work with. When was the last time you showered alone? I always know when I have drifted away from the present moment during my shower because I will have no idea if I have put the conditioner in my hair yet. Well, how could I? I was in the middle of a meeting. There are many days when I am very relieved that I shaved my legs and not my head.

Be On A Vacation

If you didn't relate to that earlier part of the book about having a quiet mind when you are away on a holiday, then may I suggest that when you are on vacation, check and see if you are actually on that vacation. If it's too tough to let go of what you left behind or you're spending the whole time worrying about the stuff you have to do when you get home, then at least have some fun with it. Send some postcards to your friends that say, "*Having a great time. Wish I was here*."

Be careful of the negative stories you tell yourself; however, feel free to tell yourself as many positive stories as you want. Sure, they may be an imagined truth that distorts your reality, but the difference is they create positive feelings rather than negative ones. Go for it. Say all kinds of fabulous things to yourself and believe every word of it. When I'm in a taxi, I pretend I have just called for my car and I'm with my personal driver – who just happens to have amnesia so he doesn't remember who I am.

Thirteen

Why It Is Best To Always Be The Hero (The Fine Art Of Re-Framing Your Struggles)

Whatever is going on in your life right now – setbacks, slowdowns, complications, heart ache or frustrations (call me psychic) – rather than resisting and resenting the challenges, view them as a quest you have been sent on, like a character in Camelot. See yourself as the intrepid and brave soul who has been selected to conquer a fierce dragon. However, in your case, it's not a dragon, it's this thing that's bringing you down.

Michelle's Epic Clash With Her Nasty, Noisy Neighbours

Doug's Great Battle With The Supervisor From Hell

Karen's Grand Voyage To A Smaller Waist Size

Oh yes, your journey is one that will inspire many as your tale of perseverance is told to both the young and old.

Re-frame. Tell yourself a story that works for you rather than against you. When dramatic flair comes with a positive spin, embellishing the facts is quite an acceptable and worthy endeavour.

Whatever it is that is stressing you out, or making you wish the "escape" button on your keyboard offered more power than it does, see it as a great adventure and choose to be the fearless hero who not only welcomes the challenge, but knows they will rise...and shine brighter because of it.

You'll find that the bigger the challenge is, the better legend it makes.

Always be the hero.

You are so the chosen one.

You are always at the right place at the right time.

Everything takes work – the stuff that lifts you up and the stuff that brings you down. Being angry, telling someone to stick it where the sun don't shine, and resenting your boss is work just like believing in yourself, doing yoga, or making someone's day. It all requires your energy and time, so why not choose the stuff that offers you the biggest return on that investment?

Fourteen

Keep Your Eyes Off The Prize: Positive Psychology 101

What would it take? What would have to happen for you to relax more, laugh more, and have more fun?

What are you waiting for? What is that thing you think will make you happy? What do you see as being the "magic key" that will unlock the door to the good life? You know, that thing. If you achieve it, acquire it, earn it, or experience it, you will totally be less bitchy. Maybe it's a promotion, maybe it's a bigger house, maybe it's a new romantic relationship, maybe it's more money, or maybe it's something else. What are you waiting for that you think will make you happier?

It's not uncommon to place happiness on the other side of success. The idea that outcomes will make us happy is perpetuated all over the place – we hear that message from all kinds of people and it's used quite effectively in the marketing and advertising world to persuade us into buying things we don't need. Beer commercials time and time again show us that if we buy this beer, we will not only be happier, but we'll also be more popular, and better looking. And of course, we'll be hanging out on a dock on a sunny day with all our beautiful friends.

In both his smash-hit TED Talk and his book, *The Happiness Advantage*, positive psychology expert, Shaw Achor, (who is clearly a favourite reference of mine) explains that to have happiness on the other side of success is setting ourselves up for an impossible task because our brains never get there. Due to our human nature and our insatiable desire to do more and get more, success tends to be a moving target. When you have a goal, the moment you achieve it, acquire it, earn it, or experience it, you immediately want something else. You get a job and then you want a better job. You earn this much money, but you want to earn more money. You get a car and then you want a nicer car. You reach your "goal weight" and then you want to lose more weight or get stronger. We have this constant desire to raise the bar higher. The moment we cross the "finish line", we put a new goal in its place. The belief that arriving at a certain outcome improves our mindset is not working for us because we never get to the place that we think will make us happy.

Our perpetual state of striving for more or better always leaves us wanting more. We are never as happy as we think we are going to be when we achieve, acquire, earn, or experience what we were aiming for. We could be revelling in the glory that be, but our state of mind is unchanged because we're already focusing on the next goal.

Think of the goals you have reached in your life. Do you remember how before those dreams came true, when you were pushing, reaching, striving, hoping, wishing, and praying, you would think to yourself, "*When this happens, I'll laugh more, I'll relax more, I'll have more fun.*"

It sure is tough to keep those promises, hey?

Don't worry, it is our human nature to not keep that promise, but being aware that you can't keep that promise is the first step toward changing how you approach the relationship between success and happiness.

As I discovered in my research into positive psychology and a wee bit of neuroscience, we have the order of things screwed up. Based on how our brains really work, it's far more effective (and realistic) to just be happy now rather than hinge your happiness on an outcome. Rather than success turning to happiness, the opposite it actually true. Our happiness can lead to success.

Neuroscience has proven that our brains have the ability to change based on our perceptions and thoughts. With a positive mindset, our brains get re-shaped and re-wired in ways that raise our productivity and performance levels. You can probably remember lots of times when you were in a good mood and while you were in that positive mindset, you were some version of unstoppable. We tend to fulfill our potential when we're happy because the overall function of our brain is more efficient – new neurons are created, new neuropathways and connections are formed, areas of the brain grow, and communication systems speed up.

As Shawn Achor says, "*Happiness is the pre-cursor for success, not the result.*"

If attaining goals doesn't make you happier, but being happier helps you attain your goals, then the million dollar question is: How can you be happy for no good reason at all?

How can you be happy right now in this moment detached of any goals being reached?

Intrinsic endeavours such as play, social interaction, gratitude, helping others, and meditation have the power to create happiness because you're doing them for their own sake.

Remember that thing you thought would help you relax more, laugh more, and have more fun? What positive psychology wants you to consider is that you will achieve it, acquire it, earn it, or experience it far easier and far faster when you start by relaxing more, laughing more, and having more fun.

Isn't it cool how the unexpected changes in your life bring about things you would never have dreamt up on your own?

See no problems – only challenges that will be seen as a sacred gift someday. Maybe even today.

Fifteen

Crisis or Opportunity? It Depends On How You Look At It...

The Chinese character used for the word, "crisis", is the same character used for the word, "opportunity". When I discovered that fact, I thought it was rather appropriate because those two experiences are synonymous. As I scan my life for those times when the !@#$ hit the fan, I see how it was also some sort of opportunity for me to shift, grow, and expand in some way. As I stood among the ashes, there was an opportunity to rise up.

When you look back and see the times in your life that you considered a "crisis", can you also see the many and varied opportunities you received to change your mind, correct your thinking, or see things in a new way?

Losing your job is an opportunity to take a risk or live more authentically.

Being in a toxic relationship is an opportunity to love yourself enough to get the hell out.

Experiencing illness or an injury is an opportunity to see how strong you really are.

Falling on hard financial times is an opportunity to be aware of, and grateful for, the abundance that does exist in your life.

A loved one dying is an opportunity to recognize the power in enjoying the life you have.

Because the words, "crisis" and "opportunity" truly are one and the same, in my efforts to see the lighter side of life, I've decided to only use the positive word.

Try it!

When things get really hectic at work, put that positive spin on things and say, "*I can't cope with one more opportunity today. Every day it's just one more opportunity after another.*" And if you have a teenager, you can switch the words in your head as you're hearing them being uttered. The next time your teenage son or daughter is having a "moment", all you will hear is, "*Mom! Dad! You don't understand! I'm dealing with a major opportunity right now!*"

See? Much better.

"We see things as we are, not as they are."

- Leo Rosten

People are always doing their very best based on what they know and what they have experienced so far.

Sixteen

Seeing The "Good" In Everyone

"When I'm having trouble with someone, it's a sure sign that person is exactly the gift I am needing in my life. Sometimes it takes me years to write the thank you note, though."

- Unknown

Whether it's an annoying co-worker, a meddling mother-in-law, or a nasty neighbour, the people in our lives who challenge us the most can make the storyline in the movie, "Castaway", (being all alone on an island talking to a volleyball) seem very attractive. What can change that temptation to run away and hang out with piece of sports equipment into gratitude? My advice is to see the "good" in everyone.

Yes, I know that people have been known to lie, cheat, and steal, but there is "good" in everyone. While it may be challenging to love some people in the midst of their humanity, it is that very challenge (and opportunity) to love that is the “good” in everyone.

Love is why you are here in the first place and the many ways that people open your heart, teach you to love, and show you the capacity you have for love are how you fulfill your life’s purpose. The “good” in everyone is how everyone shows up for your “higher good”.

When we first arrive at the beginning of our lives, loving everything and everyone is easy because it is in our nature. As time goes by, our head gets filled with beliefs and thoughts that turn love into a tougher task. The way everyone serves our higher good is that they help us to see what we have yet to let go of to be that loving being we first showed up as at the beginning of our lives. Uttering the words, “*I’ll never do that again.*” or “*I’ll never be like that again.*” is a sign that something that has been keeping our heart closed is on its way out.

Love is compassionate. Has anyone ever taught you to live with less judgement and to love people despite your differences?

Love is patient and peaceful. Has anyone ever taught you to live with less expectations and accept and love people exactly as they are?

Love is kind and generous. Has anyone ever taught you to live with less self-importance and to express love by helping someone else?

Love is unconditional. Has anyone ever taught you to live with less standards about who you love and to choose love because that is ultimately your #1 job in life?

Love wants the best for you and lifts you up. Has anyone ever taught you to love yourself enough to leave a relationship that isn't loving?

As I look back on my life, I can clearly see that those people in both my professional and personal life who brought about frustration, tears, and more phone calls to my mother than I would like to admit, were just doing their jobs – they stopped me in my tracks – they widened my eyes – they gave me a reality check – they showed me stuff I hadn't yet let go of.

Did it hurt? Hell, yeah. Did it suck? Big time. Did it rock my world just when it needed rocking in that certain way? Yes and yes. And now I could send each of them a rather lengthy thank-you note.

These lessons may come in the form of an annoying co-worker, a meddling mother-in-law, or a nasty neighbour, but always remember – the Universe only sends us angels.

One of my favourite authors, Dr. Wayne Dyer, once pointed out that inside the word, "tormentor", lies the word, "mentor". Can you see that? Not literally of course as it's clearly the last two syllables of the word. However, can you see that with every encounter, you have, in some way, "met your match"? Can you see that you have found a teacher?

There are two tricks the Universe has to help us see the "good" in everyone. When we don't learn the lessons that are offered to us, the same teacher will keep returning with new names in different contexts until we get it. The second trick is that we will be stuck with certain teachers for almost our entire lives because their lesson is very hard for us to learn and those teachers are our relatives.

The term, "soul mate", is often used to describe someone who we feel is "the one" and who will be with us forever. While finding and being with "the one" is a beautiful and purposeful part of the human experience, it is those who hurt us, leave us, and have us consider switching teams who are also our "perfect match". The people we don't stay with tend to be the ones who send us the biggest messages. The ones that are hard to ignore. The ones that are big, neon signs that can't help but show us what we have yet to let go of to reclaim the loving nature with which we first showed up. Our "soul mates" are who our souls evolve from the most. And often, it's our "soul mates" who prepare us well to meet "the one".

The reason some relationships end is the same reason anything ends – it's time to take the next step along your journey and experience a new adventure that will give you a chance to be more loving than you ever have been before. Whether it's being alone, or with someone else, happier days are always ahead. Maybe not tomorrow, but in the not too distant future. Find the trust in that by looking back and seeing how your life has always been bettering itself.

Think of that big break up. You know, the one when you didn't get out of your pyjamas or engage in much hygiene for weeks. The one when your friends would call, but you didn't answer the phone because you didn't want them to interrupt your malaise or make you start feeling anything other than the numbness that was weirdly working for you. The one when you played that sappy song over and over again because that one line totally nailed the hell you were going through. The one when cereal was an acceptable form of dinner for more nights than you would like to admit. You know, the one when you thought you would never get over it or love again? Right, that one. Now, I want you to think of all the reasons you are so damn glad you never ended up marrying that one.

Yes, there is "good" in everyone.

Try smiling at everyone you see at work, on the street, at the mall, or on the bus like they are all Buddhas teaching you something about love. You may very well freak them out, but if someone smiles back then that's a fairly good indication that they see the "good" in you.

I once had this friend who was really frustrated with someone struggling to find the courage to end an unhealthy relationship. Even though this person told my friend that she was trying her best, my friend couldn't understand her difficulty. My friend said to me, "*I try to have compassion for her, but I know that I am judging her in this situation.*" I then smiled and said to my friend, "*So, it seems that you want to have compassion for her, but you are struggling to do that? Does that mean you're trying your very best?*"

Have you ever noticed how many of your wishes have been fulfilled?

Seventeen

Do You See The Magic Even When Things Don't Seem So Magical?

As the good times roll, you get that job, you fall in love, you win that prize, or you reach that goal, doesn't life seem magical? As events unfold at the perfect time in the perfect way and the perfect people cross your path in the perfect way at the perfect time, you feel that life is on your side and you can sense the angels flitting about conspiring on your behalf. All is right with the world.

When you lose that job, your rear-end gets dumped, you can't win for losing, or success keeps eluding you, does life still seem magical? As your plans go out the window, your dreams are dashed, or your marriage goes up in smoke, do you still feel like life is on your side and do you sense the angels flitting about conspiring on your behalf? When things don't seem so magical, do you choose to see the magic anyway?

When you start thinking that nothing is going your way, keep in mind that is precisely the only thing that is happening. Nothing is going *your way* – the way you expected, the way you had planned, or the way you think is best. As you face some sort of "rough patch" in life, things may not be going *your* way, but things are still going some way. If nothing is going, that means you cease to exist, which is probably much bigger trouble than things not going your way.

As long as you are alive (and I actually believe even when you're not), you're always on the grid and where ever you are on the grid, you have been lovingly moved there along a path containing adventures that have been well-planned, well-timed, and well-orchestrated on your behalf.

As long as you are on the grid, there is nothing out of order and nothing is random.

When nothing goes your way, can you trust (or heck, even know) that there is a path unfolding that has your very best interests in mind? Even though things aren't going according to "plan", can you spot any evidence that shows you that very same magic is still swirling about?

Do you still notice that events are unfolding at the perfect time in the perfect way and the perfect people are crossing your path in the perfect way at the perfect time?

Can you see that life is still on your side?

Can you still sense the angels conspiring on your behalf?

I know that life delivers some real doozies that can make your world feel like it's been put in an industrial strength blender and I know there are times when you think you can't face one more day, but when you notice everyday miracles, it's a way of remembering that things simply aren't going your way. While it contradicts what you had in mind, you are still being lovingly guided along your path. When you see tiny bits of magic, you know you're still on the grid.

A coincidence is an everyday miracle. I was hired to speak at an International Women's Day event and didn't have a clue about how I was going to tailor a speech to mark the occasion. I write and speak about mindfulness, not women's studies. During the few weeks leading up to the event, my partner attended a conference that featured a speaker who spoke about the difference between the male and female brains. I was inspired to buy the book and learn more. To my delight, the book explained why men and women deal with stress differently based on the designs of their brains. Bingo! I shared this research in my speech and linked it to how women can heal their predispositions to chronic stress through mindfulness. Call it a coincidence (or a "synchronicity"), but I also see pure magic.

A happy surprise is an everyday miracle. At one point in my life when money was rather tight, I was in clothing store and decided to buy a pair of jeans. The cost of the jeans was a rather good deal so I felt pretty good about the decision to purchase them. When it was time to pay, the lady who was helping me said, "*That's five dollars and seventy-nine cents.*" I looked at her with both confusion and shock. She explained to me that the jeans had a particular code on the price tag that provided a significant discount on top of the already low price. She said nothing about why the jeans were less expensive than a latte at Starbucks, but it was a delightful and timely surprise. Call it a happy surprise, but I also see pure magic.

A stroke of good luck is an everyday miracle. I practice yoga a few times a week at a studio here in downtown Toronto. This studio just happens to be located on a street where there is always street parking available and it's reasonably priced. This significantly helps make yoga a habit in my life which is not only good for my health but a constant source of inspiration for the work that I do. And, if you know Toronto at all, then you know that the chances of finding available and affordable parking are very slim. Call it good luck, but what I also see pure magic.

A kind gesture is an everyday miracle. One morning I was watching The Morning Show on Global TV and one of the show's hosts, Rosey Edeh, was talking about how men and women deal with stress differently. As I had just written a blog post about based on similar brain research that I just read, I sent a "tweet" to Rosey with a link to my blog post. Rosey was kind enough to "re-tweet" that link to all of her followers which was great exposure for my blog. Call it a kind gesture, but what I also see is pure magic.

Perfect timing is an everyday miracle. I was writing this chapter that very morning I was watching The Morning Show and as I was trying to come up with an example from my life that would illustrate a kind gesture, an email from Twitter notifying me of Rosey's "re-tweet" appeared in my inbox. Call it perfect timing, but what I also see is pure magic.

When things don't go your way, can you still see how these everyday miracles prove that nothing is out of order, that you are still on the "grid" and that there is still magic swirling around you just like when the good times roll, you get that job, you fall in love, you win that prize, or you reach that goal?

These everyday miracles can be very small in nature, but they are not subtle in their power. In fact, it's because of magic like good luck, happy surprises, and perfect timing that the good times start rolling, you get that job, you find that love, you win that big prize, or reach that goal.

You always know what to do. You may not like your options. You may be paralyzed by fear. You may not want to admit it. But one thing is for sure, you always know. The trick is to act on that wisdom with unwavering faith that the Universe has your back. And here's the good news – the Universe does have your back.

You can't please everyone or make everyone happy. You can't even please or make most people happy. This has nothing to do with you – most people are not pleased or happy.

Eighteen

Leave The Rescuing To The Cops, Firefighters, And Lifeguards

Giving unsolicited advice.

Stepping in.

Taking over.

Speaking up or standing up for someone else.

Paying someone else's bills.

As you lay awake late at night or pace your kitchen floor thinking about what someone should be doing to get themselves out of a bind or back on track, you are spending time in another person's business. As you swoop in and try to make everything all better, you are spending time in another person's business. Involving yourself in other people's business is what my friend and fellow author and speaker, Rosita Hall, refers to as “second-hand stress”.

Now, as you know, I don’t believe stress actually works that way. You can’t inhale stress or catch it like a virus, but you can find yourself fretting as you dwell on or involve yourself in someone else’s business.

It may come with the shiny facade of concern, support, or generosity, but trying to rescue someone is an act of interference. When we get in there and start fretting and trying fix things, we are interfering with someone’s sacred path. We’re coming along and messing with a situation that has been perfectly planned, timed, and orchestrated on behalf of that person’s evolution.

I know it’s tough to watch from the sidelines, but in the midst of the chaos, there is actually nothing out of order. That person’s setback or screw-up is a perfectly positioned and pivotal point along their journey that will lead them to taking the next step.

Trust that there is nothing going wrong. If you need help trusting that, simply look back and see how the challenges in your life ended up to be the “wake-up call”, the “a-ha moment”, the “rock bottom”, that lifted you up. When you allow the people around you to fall down or flail about, you’re giving them the chance to receive that same gift of growth.

Staying out of people's business is not only good for your state of mind, it helps the souls around you do what they came here to do.

As lovely as your help may seem, and as good as your intentions may be, it's not your job to rescue anybody. In fact, you are best serving those around you by making your job to let it be. It's your job to listen. It's your job to empathize. It's your job to cheer them on. It's your job to say a little prayer for them. It's your job to love them deeply and unconditionally. It's your job to be patient and trust that the Universe knows exactly what it's doing.

Just like light houses don't hurl themselves into the stormy waters to grab each boat they see, shine your light brightly and let it comfort and guide those around you.

Resist the urge to dive in and pull people safely to shore.

Jumping in to save the day only robs someone of a lesson that was meant especially for them.

Of course, there is a place for rescuing people in this world. If someone is in physical danger, bring on the rescuing! But let's leave the rescuing to the cops, the firefighters, and the lifeguards. The rest is none of our business.

Stressed because you need something that you don't have? Have you ever considered that if you truly needed it, you would have it? Timing is everything and there is a natural order to it all. You always have everything you need for the particular point you are at in your journey. If, and when, something or someone new will serve your higher good, it, or they, will arrive at the perfect time. What is missing from most people's lives is the realization that nothing is missing.

Nineteen

Seeing Struggle As The Required Tension In Your Life

"The world is the great gymnasium where we come to make ourselves strong."

- Swami Vivekananda,
Indian Philosopher and Spiritual Leader

Getting dumped. Losing your job. Being broke. With life comes struggle. To know that truth, to be aware of it, and to accept it is where grace (and sanity) lies.

To celebrate struggle is another thing. That kind of positive attitude takes gratitude.

Being grateful for your struggles comes from understanding that your struggles are pieces of tension that are required in your life to push you beyond your comfort zone and pull you aside to show you something you need to see about yourself or something you have yet to let go.

Every living thing on this planet experiences struggle and every living thing on this planet gains its power and strength from struggle.

Every living thing on this planet needs struggle to evolve.

You know what you know and you can do what you do thanks to struggle.

A hawk's struggle for food is how the hawk can spot and follow a mouse scurrying hundreds of feet below on the ground. You don't get "hawk eye" from hittin' a drive thru.

A mouse's struggle to stay alive is the very thing that helps it develops its speed and agility. Running for your life can transform you into quite an athlete.

Just like the struggle between the hawk and mouse, your struggles are the pieces of tension that you need to push and pull you into deciding, declaring, and experiencing who you *really* are.

Longing for something helps you develop patience.

Being pressured to do something helps you develop authenticity.

Being bullied helps you establish boundaries.

Facing uncertainty helps you strengthen faith.

Experiencing change helps you develop adaptability and flexibility.

Managing imperfection helps you foster compassion.

Your imperfection helps you develop vulnerability.

A loss helps you develop resiliency.

Falling short helps you develop perseverance.

Be aware of how struggle has provided you with enough tension to strengthen a part of yourself

Can you see struggle as another word for, "growth"?

As a struggle throws you up in the air, tosses you about, and lands you a bit further along in your journey, wiser than you were before, it can be seen as good news when you realize that you never have nor will you ever have to sit there racking your brain trying to come up with a way to expand your consciousness or experience personal transformation. "*Man, I gotta come up with a way to evolve!*" has said no one ever.

Rejection is the Universe's way of protecting you. Whenever you are denied something, that something is not happening for a very good reason. And one day you will be grateful.

When you don't get to go where you want to be, or when you don't get what you want to have, there is simply more to gain by not going there or not having that. If and when going there or having that serves your higher good, then you will go there or have that. Timing. Is. Everything.

Twenty

Try Giving Up All Hope

Hope gets a great deal of good publicity. At face value, to hope indicates an intrepid spirit who is relentless in their pursuit of happiness. We are taught that it's the one thing we will always have and to never give it up. It even floats.

It may come with a much shinier facade, but hope is actually just another form of resistance. To hope is to want something to be different than it is.

Hoping is a euphemism for worrying. "*I hope things work out.*" It sounds better and it gets much better press, but it's really just a socially accepted way to fret.

To have hope makes it sound like you've gone and chosen a positive mindset, but it is actually desire drenched in expectation. "*This should not be happening so something else better come along to make it far more acceptable.*"

Hope is an attachment. "*I need this to happen. If it doesn't happen, that means my life is officially headed into a downward spiral.*"

Hope is like a prayer with an underlying conditional offer. "*I hope this happens. (...because I'll only be happy if it does).*"

We humans love hoping for something better; in fact, we appear to be addicted to hope. Count how many times you refer to hope in a day. Then count how many times someone else does. The trick will be to not lose track.

To live with more ease, consider giving up all hope. End all hope. Give up hope for Lent. Let go of hope and replace it with belief. Believe that the Universe knows exactly what it's doing and that it doesn't make mistakes.

Rather than hope, know that nothing is wrong and nothing is out of order. Trust that no matter what happens, you are being lovingly guided along a path that has your very best interests in mind.

Rather than hope, have faith that no matter what happens, life is always bettering itself.

Dreaming is wonderful. Send out your big, beautiful intentions and desires to the Universe and then allow life to unfold. Rather than hope for this one, very particular outcome, stay completely open to what takes place.

Giving up hope is not giving up. Giving up hope is giving up the need to control. When there is no hope, there is no reach and grasping – there is no needing a certain outcome because all outcomes are welcome.

And then, just think how much fun it will be to tell people that you are completely hopeless while wearing a big ol' grin on your face.

Life is one big play. Each moment is well-planned, well-timed, and well-orchestrated to further the development of the characters.

Twenty-One

What If Life Was A Game? (Life Viewed Through The Lens Of A Spiritual Warrior)

What if life was actually just a game?

What if you were a divine being (a soul) having a human experience, who agreed to come down here and exist in physical form to play the game?

And what if the game was a series of tests, adventures, and quests that have been strategically placed to help you complete a mission?

What if the mission was as simple as facing those challenges and choosing to love yourself and all others throughout it all?

What if being a bright light (unto the darkness) in the world was the mission?

What if being a source of unconditional love (and living out the mission) was why you showed up here in the first place?

What if remembering your mission (why you showed up here in the first place) was the thing that mattered most in life?

What if completing the mission was as simple as remembering that everyone and everything comes your way at a specific time in a specific way to help you complete the mission?

Now, what if the Universe was helping you to complete the mission? What if you and the Universe were a team? What if the Universe was orchestrating all your opportunities to complete the mission?

Rather than shaking your fist at the darkness, what about being a light unto the darkness?

What if the Universe was moving mountains for you to express the highest version of yourself so you can be a boundless source of love and light in the world?

What if the highest expression of yourself isn't someone who accomplishes great things, achieves success, and saves the world, but actually is someone who (despite life's challenges) is happy, fulfilled, and having more fun than a kid on Christmas morning?

What if you were here on the Universe's behalf so it would know itself (love) in physical form?

What if you were an ambassador of love? What if you trusted that your teammate was always on your side (this game isn't like "Survivor") and doing everything in its power to ensure that you complete the mission?

What if knowing this, and trusting that your teammate knows exactly what he or she is doing when the setbacks come along, is the very thing that helps you the most to complete the mission?

If life was a game (and of course, I'm just saying "if"), then what would the rules be?

What would help you, the spiritual warrior, to "win" the game? And by "win", I mean complete the mission – remembering what matters most – why you're here in the first place.

Would choosing to accept yourself for who you are and everyone around you for who they are help? And while we're at it, would accepting all the encounters, events, and adventures that come your way help too?

Would it help to know that who you are, and who they are, and what is happening, are all necessary parts of the game?

Would choosing compassion over judgement help? It might if everyone else is here on the same mission and at times flailing about trying to remembering why they're here in the first place. What if some folks have better memories than others?

Would staying out of people's business and allowing them to experience what is necessary for them to complete their mission be a good move? Good moves always come in handy when you're playing a game.

Would seeing all the relationships in your life as steps toward completing the mission help you get better at the game? And while we're at it, when someone is unkind, mean-spirited, and all around un-loving towards you or anyone else, would it help you complete the mission if you were able to remember that they have simply forgotten that they are here to complete the very same mission?

Would being generous in all sorts of ways be the easiest and quickest way to "win" the game? Would it help to know that the Universe promises to give you lots more of what you are giving away because it's so excited that it's getting to help people through your abundance?

Would seeing problems, challenges, and setbacks as part of the game help you play the game? What if you knew that the valleys were strategically placed for you to learn lessons, let go of beliefs, and experience adventures that will help you complete the mission?

And what if everything going on around you was lovingly sent your way to help you make your next move?

What if things don't happen *to you*, but rather, they happen *for you*?

That would make everything look less random and far more divine, yes? If you were seeing life through the lens of a spiritual warrior, there wouldn't be much to fret about and fear, yes? Wouldn't this be quite helpful if you were interested in playing the game and completing the mission?

Hmmmmm....

Game on?

“The true journey of discovery consists not in seeking new landscapes but in having fresh eyes.”

- Marcel Proust

In Gratitude...

Thank you to my friends and family for their support while I have written and published two books over the past 3 years. And by support I mean listened to me talk incessantly about how gruelling revisions are and by understanding I mean not judging me too harshly for hunching over my laptop for two summers in a row. I promise to take a break now.

A special thank you to my father, Bill, who has loved the title of this book since day 1 and asked me how the book was coming along during every phone conversation we have had over the past several months. What ever will we talk about now? Oh right, curling season is starting! ;)

Thank you to my dear friend, Heather Manning, who so graciously agreed to design the cover of this book while still recovering from working on the last book with me. God love you. I promise to leave you alone for a while now.

Thank you to Shana McEachren for editing and formatting this book. I am so lucky that my person is the most clever woman I know.

Thank you to my soul-sister and mentor, Kelly Elson. I soak up your wisdom, guidance, and light every chance I get. Thank goodness for Facebook during those months when Highway 21 is closed most days.

Thank you to Christine Alevizakis who inspired my chapter on struggle being the required tension in our lives and who gave me the analogy of the mouse and the hawk. I trust I did it justice.

Thank you to Terry, Darcy, and John at Ball Media Group for being such great team mates and for getting this book produced and into my hot little hands in time for my first speaking engagement of the fall season. We did it again! :)

And thank you to John Parkin, author or *f**k it, the ultimate spiritual way, (I highly recommend this book!)* for your ideas that have inspired me greatly as an author and a human being trying to lighten the f**k up.

Website: www.susanstewart.ca

Email: susan@susanstewart.ca

Twitter: @SusanIStewart

Facebook: Susan Stewart (author)

Find links to Susan's LinkedIn page and YouTube
channel on the homepage of www.susanstewart.ca

Register for Susan's newsletter and/or subscribe to her
blog on the homepage of www.susanstewart.ca

Invite Susan to bring
some laughter and light to an event.

You can take the girl out of stand-up comedy, but...